Vermont. Congregational church Springfield

Historical manual of the Congregational church

in Springfield, Vt., July. 1869

Vermont. Congregational church Springfield

Historical manual of the Congregational church
in Springfield, Vt., July. 1869

ISBN/EAN: 9783337374815

Printed in Europe, USA, Canada, Australia, Japan

Cover: Foto ©Lupo / pixelio.de

More available books at **www.hansebooks.com**

HISTORICAL MANUAL

OF THE

Congregational Church,

IN

SPRINGFIELD, VT.

JULY, 1869.

HISTORICAL MANUAL

OF THE

Congregational Church,

SEPTEMBER BULLETIN.

—◦◦❋◦◦——

First Church of Christ,

MAIN STREET,

SPRINGFIELD, - VERMONT.

PASTOR.

THOMAS MASON BOSS.

PARSONAGE, Pleasant Street.
At home for Religious Conversation,
Monday evenings, 7.30-8.30.
PASTOR'S RECEPTION, TUESDAY EVENING.

DEACONS.

ASHBEL STEELE,   AMASA WOOLSON,
GEO. P. HAYWOOD,   ADNA BROWN.

BRETHREN OF CHURCH COMMITTEE.

HENRY CLOSSON,   FREDERIC L. SMALL.

Non Church goers Cordially Invited.
"Come thou with us and we will do you good."

A. F. SSETT, PRINTER, SPRINGFIELD, VT.

HISTORICAL MANUAL

OF THE

Congregational Church,

Meeting for Social Worship,

FRIDAY, 7.30, P. M.

Not forsaking the assembling of ourselves togeth-
er, as the manner of some is. Heb. 10: 25.

Sept. 6th. Obedience the condition of spiritual en-
            largement. John 14: 15-25.
  " 13th. The Witnessing Church. Is. 43: 10. 44: 8.
            Acts 1: 8. 4: 33.
  " 20th. Stumbling Blocks Removed. Is. 57: 14.
            Rom. 14: 13.
  " 27th. Earnestness. Eccl. 9: 10.

Be at the Prayer Meeting without fail, unless the
Lord requires you elsewhere.
  Be punctual. Come to the front. Come in a
prayerful spirit. Be ready to take part early, by
prayer, testimony, song, incident, or text, as the
Spirit suggests. Be cheerful, uncomplaining, en-
courage others to attend and to participate. Help
make a " live meeting " by prayerful attention and
appropriation as well as regular attendance.

  " Ye shall seek me and find me, when ye shall
search for me with all your heart."

Sunday School.

Committee—The PASTOR, OTTO DOUBLEDAY,
ZIMRI MESSINGER, GEO. A. DAVIS.
Superintendent—FREDERIC L. SMALL.
Assist. Supt.—BENJ. F. ALDRICH.
Secretary and Treasurer—GEO. A. DAVIS.
Librarian—CHAS. S. HEMENWAY.

  Teacher's Meeting every Friday in the Chapel, at
8.30, P. M.

HISTORICAL MANUAL

OF THE

𝕮𝖔𝖓𝖌𝖗𝖊𝖌𝖆𝖙𝖎𝖔𝖓𝖆𝖑 𝕮𝖍𝖚𝖗𝖈𝖍,

IN

SPRINGFIELD, VT.

JULY, 1869.

"Thy vows are upon me, O God."—*Ps.* lxvi. 12.

———●———

CLAREMONT, N. H.:

PRINTED BY THE CLAREMONT MANUFACTURING CO.

1869.

HISTORICAL SKETCH.

I.

ORGANIZATION.

The Congregational Church in Springfield, Vt. was organized Oct. 3, 1781. It consisted of " eight males and eight females." From the best information we can obtain, the first sixteen in the accompanying Catalogue were the original members. The first volume of the Church Records having been lost, we have laid under tribute the Records of the Town and the memories of several of the oldest, and many of the younger inhabitants, now living, and hope the attempt here made, to rescue and preserve the names of the members, and the early history of the Church, may not result in the publication of more errors than facts. Painful search has been made to obtain what is reliable.

May 18, 1803, a Religious Society was formed to act in connection with the Church, for the support of the gospel. Prior to that time, the Town, as such, had acted with the Church, for that purpose.

II.

MEETING-HOUSES.

Jan. 4, 1786, the Town voted "to build a Meeting-House, 56x40, with posts 21 feet high, with two porches, one at each end, 12 feet square, near the Burying ground, on Hubbard's or Martin's land ; the cost of said Meeting-House to be paid in Neat Cattle or Grain at half price." Voted also, " to class the Town, and see that each class furnish its share of stuffs for building and finishing the Meeting-House."

These votes, so far, at least, as the location of the Meeting-House was concerned, were reconsidered, a part of the people of the Town preferring to locate it near the Eureka School-House, on land now owned by Abijah Miller, Esq.; others wishing to locate it on land near Mr. Christopher Ellis'; and others, where it was eventually located, on the Common, near the Village Cemetery. It was not finished till 1798.

For thirty-one years it continued to be the place "whither the tribes went up."

In 1832, a new House of Worship was built on Main Street, in the village, and dedicated Jan. 9, 1833.

In 1868, this House, having been considered, for a long time, too small conveniently to accommodate those desiring to worship in it, was enlarged, and remodeled by the addition of a Tower in front; a Chancel and Orchestra; the entire refitting of the Lecture Rooms; and the reseating of the Audience Room, with curved pews.

The cost of these improvements, including a new Organ, Communion Service, Pulpit, and Furniture, was about $14,000.

It was rededicated May 30, 1869.

III.

MINISTERS.

The first record we have of any action on the part of the Town in reference to preaching, is found in a "Notification" of a Town meeting called May 5, 1788; which was "to see if the Town will hire preaching." An affirmative vote was passed which resulted in hiring Rev. Samuel Cotton to preach three months. At the end of that time, Aug. 4, 1788, the Town "chose a Committee to join a Committee of the Church, to treat with Rev. Mr. Cotton on terms of Settlement." On the first Tuesday in September following, the Town gave Mr. Cotton a formal call. He preached for them about one year in all; but the call was declined.

So far as any record appears, the Church was without stated preaching for more than two years. May 17, 1792, a Committee was chosen by the Town, "to procure a Congregational preacher, of the standing order." Probably Rev. Benj. Stone was the choice of this Committee, and we infer that his labors commenced soon after the appointment of this Committee.

Nov. 5, 1792, the Town gave Rev. Mr. Stone a call to settle, which he declined, and the Church was without preaching again for about a year and a half.

April 5, 1794, the Town voted " to hire preaching for six months." No minister's name appears on that vote.

Dec. 17, 1794, voted " to hire preaching a year." This vote probably secured the services of Rev. Joseph Prince. How long he remained is not known, nor who, if any one, supplied the pulpit, till

April 5, 1796, when the Town chose a Committee, and raised money " to hire preaching, the ensuing season." Rev. Mr. Williams is the next man named, as supplying the pulpit. He remained some five months.

After Rev. Mr. Williams, probably about the first of Jan. 1797, Rev. Archibald Campbell came, and remained some six or eight months.

The next Candidate was Rev. Nicholas B. Whitney, who probably began to preach in Sept. 1797. April 30, 1798, the Town gave Mr. Whitney " an ineffectual call." He supplied about nine months, in all.

About a year passed, when the Town, on the first Tuesday in Sept. 1799, voted a tax of one cent on a dollar, to pay for preaching.

This vote led to action which brought Pastor Smiley here. He began to preach in Springfield, in the Spring, or early Summer, of 1800. The Town voted him a call April 6, 1801; the Church, June 28, following. He accepted the call, and became the first settled Pastor, Sept. 23, 1801; all who had served before him having been Stated or Occasional Supplies. His term of service and that of the ten settled Pastors and one Acting Pastor, who have followed him, may be found on page 13.

The average length of the nine Pastorates, previous to the present, is nearly seven years. The longest, that of Pastor Smiley, was twenty-four years, one month, and nine days; the shortest, that of Rev. Mr. Haseltine, was one year and nine days.

IV.

REVIVALS.

In eighty-seven years, the Church has enjoyed seven seasons of more or less extensive revival, viz.—

1st and 2nd, In 1810, and 1821–2,	Rev. Mr. Smiley, Pastor.
3d, In 1831,	Rev. Mr. Goodman, Pastor.
4th, In 1834–5 "Burchard Revival,"	Rev. Mr. Morton, Pastor.
5th, In 1840–2,	Rev. Mr. Noble, Pastor.
6th, In 1856–7,	Rev. Mr. Giddings, Pastor.
7th, In 1867–8,	Rev. Mr. Cobb, Pastor.

Nine hundred and forty-eight, or more than three fourths of the 1226 members of this Church, have been added by Profession; 278 by Letter. More than two thirds have been added in Revivals of Religion.

V.

THE SABBATH-SCHOOL.

In the Spring of 1818, Pastor Smiley opened a Sabbath-School in his house. He continued it as long as he was Pastor; after which, it was held, for some years, in the School-House on the Common, near the Meeting-House; and then, in the Meeting-House.

The following is a list of the Superintendents, with their terms of service, as near as can now be ascertained:

Rev. R. Smiley,	1818—1825
Dea. A. Steele,	1825—1832
Dea. Nomlas Cobb,	1832—1833
Dea. A. Steele,	1833—1839
Dea. I. M. Lewis,	1839—1842
Dea. A. Bourne,	1842—1845
Dr. E. A. Knight,	1845—1851
Leverett M. Snell,	1851—1856
Henry Safford,	1856—1859
Dea. A. Steele,	1859—1863
Dea. Adna Brown,	1863—1866
Edward Ingham,	1866—1868
Dea. Adna Brown,	1868—

VI.

FORM OF ADMISSION TO THE CHURCH.

Address.

Beloved Friends: You present yourselves before God and these witnesses, to make a solemn profession of your Christian Faith, and to enter into Covenant with Christ and his Church in this place. We trust you have duly considered the nature of this profession, and the new relations you will henceforth sustain, and that you are prepared, by Divine Grace, to offer yourselves as living sacrifices, holy and acceptable to God, through Jesus Christ.

We now ask your assent to our

ARTICLES OF BELIEF.

We believe in the one only living and true God, who exists as Father, Son and Holy Ghost; that these three are one equal and infinite, in all natural and moral perfections.

We believe that God created and upholds and governs all things according to the wise and eternal counsel of his own Will, yet in perfect accordance with the free moral action of men.

We believe that the Bible is the inspired word of God, the perfect and only rule of Belief and Practice.

We believe that our First Parents were created holy; that they fell from that state by transgressing the command of God; and that in consequence of their apostasy, all their descendants are without original holiness, and alienated from God until their hearts are renewed by Divine Grace.

We believe that the Son of God took upon himself the form of man; that he died, rose again, and ascended to the right hand of the Father, where he ever liveth to make intercession for us; that by his obedience, sufferings and death, he made a complete atonement, which is the only ground of forgiveness for sin; that pardon and eternal life are sincerely offered to all, upon condition of repentance and faith in Christ; that those who repent and believe will be kept, by the power of God, through faith, unto salvation.

We believe that Christ has established a Visible Church in the world, the terms of admission to which are,—credible evidence of Regeneration by the Holy Spirit, and a Public Profession of Faith in the Redeemer; and that Baptism and the Lord's Supper are Ordinances of the Church, to be observed to the end of time.

We believe that God has appointed one day in the seven to be kept holy unto himself; and that from the Resurrection of Christ, to the end of the world, the first day of the week is the Christian Sabbath.

We believe, also, in the Resurrection of the Dead, and in a day of Final Judgment, in which all will receive according to their deeds; that the Wicked will go away into Everlasting Punishment, and the Righteous into Life Eternal.

Experimentally, we believe that God has wrought in us genuine Repentance for Sin ; that he has renewed our hearts ; that he has justified and accepted us, and sealed us heirs of heaven.

To this Confession, according to your understanding of the truth and according to your personal Faith in Christ, do you now (severally) give your cordial assent ?

[Here Baptism is to be administered, or recognized, in answer to the following question :
Do you, who have received Baptism, on the Faith of your Parents, now publicly accept, and endorse their act as your own ?]

Will you now join us in solemn

COVENANT?

In the presence of God and these witnesses, we do now avouch the Lord Jehovah, Father, Son and Holy Ghost, to be our God, the Supreme Object of our affection and our Portion forever.

We cordially acknowledge the Lord Jesus Christ to be our Redeemer, and the Holy Spirit to be our Sanctifier, Comforter and Guide.

We cheerfully devote ourselves to God in the Covenant of his Grace ; consecrating all our powers and faculties and possessions to his service and glory.

And we promise, through the assistance of his Spirit, that we will cleave to Him as our Chief Good, that we will give diligent attention and cordial support to His word and Ordinances, in secret, in the family, and in the House of God; that we will seek the interest and honor of His Kingdom; and that, henceforth, denying all ungodliness and every worldly lust, we will live soberly and righteously and godly in the world.

We do now, more especially, join ourselves to this Church, engaging to submit to its Rules of Government and Discipline,—to strive earnestly for its peace, edification and purity,—and to walk with its members in charity, fidelity and Christian watchfulness.

Do you thus solemnly covenant and promise?

We then, the members of this Church, affectionately receive you to our communion, and, in the name of Christ, declare you entitled to all the privileges of membership in the Church of God. We welcome you to this fellowship with us in the blessings of the gospel and, on our part, engage to watch over you in Christian affection and to seek your edification as long as you continue to be with us.

And now, Beloved in the Lord, let us never forget that the vows of God are upon us, and that the obligations which we have ratified and sealed, this day, are as lasting as eternity. Wherever we go, they will be with us. They will follow us to the bar of God· They will abide with us, in whatever world we may be, forever. Let it be our constant aim and earnest prayer to God, that he will help us to fulfill them.

May the Lord guide and preserve us till death, and at last receive us all to that blessed world where our love and joy shall be perfect forever, through the grace of our Lord Jesus Christ. Amen.

PRINCIPLES AND RULES OF CHURCH ORDER.

1. A Christian Church is an Association of professed followers of Christ, organized for the purpose of mutual watchfulness; the observance of the Christian Sacraments; the maintenance of Christain worship and instruction, and the extension of the Kingdom of Christ in the world. Such a body, under Christ, is fully competent to choose its officers, admit its members, administer discipline, and do all other acts necessary to the accomplishment of these objects.

2. A Church, though thus independent of external authority, is bound in relations of mutual care and communion with other Churches; and this Church, in all ordinary cases, will conform to the usages of fellowship established among Congregational Churches.

3. The permanent officers of the Church are a Pastor, or Pastors and Deacons. This Church also appoints, annually, a Clerk, a Church-Committee to examine candidates for admission, and to secure faithful attention to discipline, and a Sabbath-School Committee of three, for the supervision of the Sabbath-School.

4. The Church-Committee consists of the Pastor and the Deacons, and two other brethren, the last to be chosen annually.

5. The Sabbath-School Committee (of which the Pastor is a member, ex officio) shall, on the day they are appointed, nominate a Superintendent, Assistant-Superintendent, Secretary, Treasurer, Librarian, Assistant-Librarian, and a board of at least five more teachers than there are classes in the Sabbath-School. These nominations, if approved by the Church, shall, on or before the day of its reorganization, be presented to the Sabbath-School for its approval. This Committee shall also be responsible for the selection of all books and papers, both for study and general reading in the Sabbath-School.

6. Persons applying for admission to the Church are first examined by the Church, under the direction of the Church-Committee, and, having been propounded for at least two weeks, are admitted by vote taken at the Preparatory Lecture; and become members in full by publicly assenting to the Articles of Belief and Covenant.

7. Members of any and all other Christian Churches, worshiping with us, are cordially invited to the Lord's Table, and all other privileges of Church members, for one year. Within that time, they are specially desired to bring letters of dismission and recommendation to us, and become members with us.

8. Members of this church, removing from town to become permanent residents elsewhere, are expected to take letters of dismission from us to some church near where they reside, within the space of one year from their removal, unless they give the church satisfactory reasons for not doing so.

9. The rule of Christ, enjoined in Matt. xviii. 15--17, is to be literally followed by members of this Church in all cases of private offense, and the spirit of this rule is to govern all disciplinary processes in relation to members guilty of other offenses.

10. The Annual Meeting of the Church is on Friday preceding the first Sabbath in April.

11. The Lord's Supper is administered on the first Sabbaths, respectively, of January, March, May, July, September, and November.

Preparatory Lecture, Friday P. M. preceding Communion Sabbath.

12. The Social meetings of the Church are as follows :—

I. MONTHLY.

1. Missionary Concert, the first Sabbath of each month.
2. Social Conference, the first Monday of each month.
3. Sabbath-School Concert, the second Sabbath of each month.
4. Church-Meeting, the last Friday in each month.

II. WEEKLY.

1. Pastor's Meeting, Monday evening.
2. Young People's Prayer Meeting, Tuesday evening.
3. Ladies' Prayer Meeting, or Social Union, Wednesday afternoon.
4. Church Prayer Meeting, and Sabbath-School Teachers' Meeting, Friday evening.

BENEVOLENT CONTRIBUTIONS.

Stated Contributions, for Benevolent Objects, are taken in Church, the *first Sabbath morning of each month*, as follows :—

January ;—Poor of the Parish.
March ;—Bible Society.
May ;—Sabbath-School.
June ;—Home Missions.
July ;—Poor of the Parish.
August ;—American Missionary Association.
September :—Education Society.
October ;—Tract Society.
November ;—Seamen's Cause.
December ;—Am. Congregational Union.

In addition to the above, a Collection is taken at the Preparatory Lecture for Church Expenses; and, in *the month of January*, by special canvass, a subscription for *Foreign Missions*.

PASTOR'S REQUESTS AND APPOINTMENTS.

1. The Pastor specially desires to be informed by the persons themselves, or by others, of REMOVALS FROM TOWN, prior to their going, if possible, of any family, or individual belonging to this Church or Congregation; and of REMOVALS INTO TOWN, of any family or individual, who would choose to worship with us.

2. Members of the Church and Congregation are particularly requested to inform the Pastor, at once, of all cases of SICKNESS AND AFFLICTIONS where his counsel and sympathy may be desired.

3. Any persons, in the Church or Congregation, who desire personal RELIGIOUS CONVERSATION, with the Pastor, are cordially invited to call at his study, Monday Evening of each week, between 7 and 9 o'clock; or Friday P. M. between 2 and 4 o'clock. The Pastor would prefer in no case to receive calls in the forenoon of any day, except in case of urgent necessity.

4. Before the appointment of the hour for FUNERAL SERVICES, the Pastor asks in all cases to be consulted, as other engagements may make it impossible to attend at an hour independently chosen. It is specially requested that, when convenient, an earlier hour than one o'clock P. M. may not be chosen, and that in no case, except imperative necessity, funeral services be appointed on the Sabbath.

PASTORS.

Complete Table of Names of Pastors from the organization of the Church to 1869, with the dates of the prominent events of their lives.

No.	Name.	Birth place.	Date of Birth.	College.	Place of Theological Education. With	Date of Ordination and Installation.	Date and Mode of Removal.
1	Robinson Smiley,	Jaffrey, N. H.	Apr. 19, 1771.	D. C., 1799.	Rev.Wm.Emerson,D.D. Boston, Rev. N. Thayer, Lancaster, Ms.	Ord. September 23d, 1801.	Dism'd Oct. 26, 1825.
2	Eliaf W. Goodman,	So. Hadley, Ms.	Feb. 9, 1791.	Un. Col., 1820.	Princeton, N. J. 1823.	Ord. 1823, Ins. May 23, 1827.	Dism'd Oct. 26, 1831.
3	Daniel O. Morton,	Winthrop, Me.	Dec. 21, 1788.	M. C., 1812.	Rev. Wm. Patten, D. D.	Ord.June30,1814, Ins.May23,'32.	Dism'd Feb. 3, 1836.
4	Henry B. Holmes,	Stratford-upon-Avon, Eng.	Apr. 5, 1808.	Not a Graduate	Rev. Benjamin Holmes, Eng. His Father.	Ord. Nov. 1830, Ins. June 28, '36.	Dism'd Nov. 24, 1840.
5	Calvin D. Noble,	Chelsea, Vt.	Sept. 11, 1811.	M. C., 1834.	Rev. Willard Child and Rev. James Buckham.	Ord. June 8, 1836, Ins.Nov.24,'40.	Died Aug. 23, 1844.
6	Lathrop Taylor,	Buckland, Ms.	Aug. 3, 1813.	M. C., 1839.	Andover, 1842.	Ord. May 16, 1843, Ins. Oct. 1, '45.	Dism'd Nov. 4, 1851.
7	Solomon P. Giddings,	Poultney, Vt.	Dec. 2, 1812.	M. C., 1838.	New Haven, and Lane.	Ord. Sept. 1842, Ins. June 8, '52.	Dism'd Aug. 24, 1858.
8	Nathan J. Haseltine,	Chester, N. H.	Mar. 29, 1829.	D. C., 1855.	Andover, 1858.	Ord. and Ins. Jan. 13, 1859.	Died Jan. 29, 1860.
9	Jno. W. Chickering, Jr.	Bolton, Ms.	Sept. 11, 1831.	B. C., 1852.	Bangor, 1860.	Ord. and Ins. Sept. 19, 1860.	Dism'd Dec. 15, 1863.
10	Asa Mann, (A. P.)	Randolph, Ms.	Apr. 9, 1816.	A. C., 1838.	Andover, 1842.	Ordained June 19, 1844.	A.P.Mar.'64 to Feb.'66.
11	Levi Henry Cobb,	Cornish, N. H.	June 30, 1827.	D. C., 1854.	Andover, 1857.	Ord. Oct. 28, 1857, Ins. May 2, '67.	

TABLE OF DEACONS,

Showing the length of their terms of service.

No	Name.	Appointed.	Ceased to Act.	Remarks and References.
1	Lemuel Whitney,	Nov. 17, 1801	Feb. 1, 1813	Died.
2	Newcomb Bourne,	Nov. 17, 1801	Jan. 24, 1810	Resigned.
3	David Nichols,	June 11, 1807	Mar. 12, 1842	Died.
4	Phinehas Bates,	Apr. 17, 1811	Nov. 1, 1843	Died.
5	Joseph Selden,	Mar. 15, 1814	Dec. 22, 1855	Died.
6	Horatio G. Hawkins,	Aug. 4, 1832	Oct. 16, 1836	Left Town.
7	Elijah Whitney,	Aug. 4, 1832	April 4, 1855	Died.
8	Arba Holman,	Aug. 4, 1832	Feb. 29, 1864	Left Town.
9	Ashbel Steele,	Aug. 25, 1837	Nov. 6, 1842	Left Town.
10	Nomlas Cobb,	Aug. 25, 1837	July 27, 1838	Died.
11	Isaac M. Lewis,	Oct. 1, 1841	Nov. 29, 1866	Died.
12	Abraham J. Bourne,	Oct. 1, 1841	June 11, 1848	Left Town.
13	William Davis,	Oct. 1, 1841	Sept. 15, 1868	Died.
14	Ashbel Steele (Reappointed)	Sept. 2, 1859		
15	George P. Haywood,	Aug. 26, 1864		
16	Amasa Woolson,	June 28, 1867		
17	Adna Brown,	June 28, 1867		

EXPLANATORY NOTE.

In the following Catalogue of members, the first column numbers the members in the order of their admission. The second column contains the original and present names of all who have ever belonged to this Church. Parentheses or brackets inclose the maiden names of married females. Male Christian names, in parentheses, are those of the husbands of females whose names they follow. Female surnames in parentheses denote a second or subsequent marriage. Column third gives the dates of reception. Column fourth records the manner of reception, and the Churches from which members have been received by letter. Column fifth gives the dates of removal. Column sixth, the manner of removal, and the ages of those removed by death.

CATALOGUE OF MEMBERS.

CHRONOLOGICAL CATALOGUE OF MEMBERS,

FROM THE FORMATION OF THE CHURCH IN 1781 TO 1869.

No.	Name.	Date of Recept'n.	Manner of Reception.	Date of Removal.	Manner of Removal.
1	Lennel Whitney (Dea.)	Oct. 3, 1781	Letter from ch. in Tolland, Ct.	Feb. 1, 1813	By death, aged 71 years.
2	Thankful (Griffith) Whitney (Dea. Len.)	"	"	Feb. 24, 1818	By death, aged 72 years.
3	Newcomb Bourne (Dea.)	"	Letter from ch. in Cohasset, Ms.	April 25, 1821	By death, aged 77 years.
4	Abigail (Joy) Bourne (Dea. N.)	"	"	Feb. 18, 1839	By death, aged 92 years.
5	Simon Stevens	"	Letter from ch. in Canterbury, Ct.	Feb. 18, 1817	By death, aged 81 years.
6	Samuel Cobb (Dr.)	"	Letter from ch. in Tolland, Ct.	March 15, 1806	By death, aged 59 years.
7	Ann (Steele) Cobb (Dr. Samuel)	"	Letter from ch. in Sutton, Ms.	June 23, 1821	By death, aged 66 years.
8	Abigail (Gould) Barnard (Jona.)	"	Letter from ch. in	July 11, 1810	By death, aged 71 years.
9	Sarah Draper	"	Letter from ch. in Tolland, Ct.		By death, aged years.
10	Lucretia (Scott) Burge (Nath.)	"	Letter from ch. in Middletown, Ct.	April 6, 1847	By death, aged 88 years.
11	Simeon Spencer	"		March 23, 1808	By death, aged 69 years.
12	John Barrett (Col.)	"	Profession of Faith.	Dec. 3, 1806	By death, aged 75 years.
13	Asher Evans	"	Letter from ch. in Chelmsford, Ms.	June 15, 1813	By death, aged 45 years.
14	Hannah Walker	"	Letter from ch. in Taunton, Ms.		By death, aged years.
15	Isaac Smith	"	Letter from ch. in Cohasset, Ms.	Aug. 17, 1816	By death, aged 72 years.
16	Betsey (Stoddard) Tower (Isaac)	July 5, 1801	Letter from ch. in Langdon, N. H.	March 7, 1812	By death, aged 59 years.
17	David Rice (Capt.)	"	Letter from ch. in		By death, aged years.
18	Elihu Bascom	"	Profession of Faith.		By death, aged years.
19	Adonijah Bixby	"		March 8, 1839	By death, aged 85 years.
20	Mary (Brown) Bixby (Adonijah)	"		Sept. 19, 1830	By death, aged 70 years.
21	Elizabeth (Field) Tower (Isaac Jr.)	Sept. 23, 1801	Letter from ch. in Harvard, Ms.	March 17, 1842	By death, aged 52 years.
22	Robinson Smiley (Rev.)	Oct. 11, 1801	Profession of Faith.	June 24, 1856	By death, aged 85 years.
23	Merrill (Bates) Brown (Elisha)	"	"	Aug. 22, 1851	By death, aged 97 years.
24	Lovisa (Ward) Brown (Luke)	Jan. 24, 1802	"	Oct. 23, 1847	By death, aged 68 years.
25	Elizabeth (Harkness) Smiley (Rev. R.)	April 28, 1802		Oct. 2, 1860	By death, aged 87 years.
26	Levi Nichols		Letter from ch. in Winchendon, Ms	April 2, 1809	By death, aged 71 years.

	Name	Date admitted	Manner of admission	Date	Remarks
27	Elizabeth (Sawyer) Nichols (Levi)	April 28, 1802	Letter from ch.in Winchendon, Ms.	Jan. 15, 1813	By death, aged 70 years.
28	Priscilla (Litchfield) Whitcomb (Perez)	July 4, 1802	Profession of Faith.	July 10, 1843	By death, aged 61 years.
29	Betsey (Bates) Barrett (Thomas)	Oct. 3, "	"	Sept. 23, 1850	By death, aged 79 years.
30	Nicholas Brugg		"	Aug. 7, 1804	By death, aged 74 years.
31	Lucy (Nichols) Barnard (Jenison)	Oct. 24, 1802	"	Dec. 15, 1865	By death, aged 90 years.
32	Oliver Sartwell		"	Nov. 20, 1807	By death, aged years.
33	Hannah (Taylor) Sartwell (Oliver)	"	"	Sept. 22, 1812	By death, aged years.
34	Abner Bislee jr.	"	"	Oct. 30, 1818	By death, aged 45 years.
35	Barbara (Wilson) Bisbee (Abner jr.)	"	"	March 14, 1854	By death, aged 81 years.
36	Catharine (Nichols) Stevens (Simon jr.)	"	"	Oct. 11, 1835	Dis. to ch. in Felicity, O.
37	Mercy (Tower) (Shattuck) (Sam.jr.) Spencer (Jonas)	"	"	Dec. 4, 1856	By death, aged 77 years.
38	Betsey (Tower) Smith (Hugh)	"	"	June 10, 1858	By death, aged 73 years.
39	Lucy (Bates) Bemis (John)	Oct. 25, 1802	"	Jan. 1, 1836	Dis. to ch. in Claremont, N. H.
40	Eunice P. (Ward) Randall (Simeon)	Nov. 4, "	"	Jan. 3, 1840	By death, aged 54 years.
41	Naamah (Gilbert) Ward (Calvin)		"		By death, aged years.
42	David Nichols (Dea.)	Dec. 10, 1802	"	May 12, 1842	By death, aged 85 years.
43	Naomi (Newton) Nichols (Dea. David)		"	Aug. 19, 1837	By death, aged 76 years.
44	Lucretia (Hinckley) Nye (George)	Feb. 6, 1803	"		By death, aged years.
45	Betsey (Davis) Woodbury (John) Griswold (Daniel)	April 28, 1803	"	Oct. 26, 1803	By death, aged 67 years.
46	Abel Brown	April 28, 1803	Letter from ch. Fitzwilliam, N. H.	Feb. 18, 1827	Dis. to ch. in Parishville, N. Y.
47	Sarah (Stoddard) Brown (Abel)		Profession of Faith.	Jan. 6, 1840	By death, aged 71 years.
48	John Wilson	Aug. 4, 1803	"	Aug. 2, 1811	By death, aged 75 years.
49	Barbara (Grugg) Wilson (John)	"	"	Sept. 3, 1829	By death, aged 88 years.
50	Mary (Hall) Bisbee (Capt. Abner)	Sept. 25, 1803	"	July 6, 1862	By death, aged 78 years.
51	Miriam (Nichols) Tolles (Henry)	Feb. 25, 1804	"	Jan. 1, 1827	Dis. to ch. in Weathersfield Cen.
52	Sally Rice		"	May 4, 1810	Dis. to ch. in Whiting.
53	Eunice (Bigelow) Woodward (Sam.)	Oct. 25, 1804	"	June 1, 1842	By death, aged 84 years.
54	Eunice (Woodward) Gil son (Jonas)	Aug. 11, 1805	"	April 26, 1869	By death, aged 96 years.
55	Polly (Bixby) Blanchard (Stephen)	Sept. 8, 1805	"	April 4, 1813	By death, aged 29 years.
56	Samuel Scott	Oct. 31, 1805	Letter from ch. in Weathersfield.	Oct. 2, 1814	By death, aged 84 years.
57	Eleazer Sartwell	Dec. 1, 1805	Profession of Faith.		Dis. to ch. in
58	Hannah (Mather) Sartwell (Eleazer)	"	"		"
59	Mary (Briggs) Smith (Isaac)		"	Oct. 30, 1822	By death, aged 77 years.
60	Samuel Shattuck	Feb. 2, 1806	Letter from ch. in Pepperill, Ms.	Sept. 6, 1833	By death, aged 78 years.
61	Hannah (Hartwell) Shattuck (Sam.)	"	"	March 1, 1850	By death, aged 99 years.
62	Deborah (Hoar) Holden (Ezra)	"	Profession of Faith.		Dis. to ch. in
63	Esther (Chandler) Bates (Theophilus)	May 4, 1806	"	March 3, 1851	By death, aged 81 years.
64	Polly (Benton) Heald (Jesse)	March 15, 1807	"	Oct. 15, 1824	Dis. to ch. in Chester.
65	Sarah (Babcock) Hubbard (Capt. Lem.)	April 26, 1807	"	Sept. 12, 1824	Exc. See Church Records.
66	Samuel Cobb	May 3, 1807	"	June 30, 1809	Dis. to ch. in Lewis, N. Y.
67	Hannah (Hall) Dana (Ezra)		"	Oct. 8, 1816	Dis. to ch. in Windsor.
68	Azubah (Atwood) Howard (John)		"	May 22, 1814	

No.	Name.	Date of Recept'n.	Manner of Reception.	Date of Removal.	Manner of Removal.
69	Lydia (Spalding) Farrar (Nathaniel)	June 7, 1807	Profession of Faith.	Sept. 1, 1816	Dis. to ch. in Madrid, N. Y.
70	David Smiley	June 14, 1807	"	Aug. 8, 1830	Dis. to ch. in Danbury, N. H.
71	Mary (Harkness) Smiley (David)	"	"		
72	Phinehas Bates (Dea.)	June 30, 1807	"	Nov. 1, 1843	By death, aged 77 years.
73	Abigail (Lincoln) Bates (Dea. P.)	"	"	July 15, 1830	By death, aged 65 years.
74	Esther Cobb	July 15, 1807	"	Oct. 27, 1838	By death, aged 60 years.
75	Martha (Stoughton) Cobb (Jeduthan)	Aug. 6, 1807	"	June 22, 1845	Dis. to ch. in Westport, N. Y.
76	Sarah (Darling) Cutler (Loammi)	Nov. 1, 1807	"	Jan. 24, 1809	By death, aged 40 years.
77	James Bellows	May 1, 1808	"		By death, aged years.
78	Moses Cobb (Dr.)	"	"	June 22, 1845	Dis. to Con. ch. Kalamazoo, Mich
79	Thomas Corlew				By death, aged years.
80	Elizabeth ( ) Kanow (John)	June 7, 1808			By death, aged years.
81	Anna (Pomeroy) Hubbard (Lucius)	July 3, 1808		Jan. 4, 1839	Dis. to ch. in Chester.
82	Joseph Labaree (Rev.)	Aug. 21, 1808		May 22, 1814	Dis. to ch. in Jericho.
83	Nathan Caldwell	Sept. 2 1808		Aug. 22, 1839	By death, aged 72 years.
84	Betsey (Brown) Thompson (John S.)	"	Letter from ch. in Northfield.	Sept. 30, 1863	By death, aged 84 years.
85	Susanna (Chilson) Cook (Philip)	"	Profesion of Faith.	July 4, 1817	By death aged 33 years.
86	Deborah (Oakes) Pratt (Daniel)	July 23, 1809	"	July 14, 1856	By death, aged 79 years.
87	Lydia (Priest) Persons (Oliver)	"	"	Oct. 4, 1821	Dis. to ch. in Weston.
88	Theodocia (Nichols) Gould ( )	"	"		Dis. to ch. in Plattsburg, N. Y.
89	Sarah ( ) Priest (*)	Aug. 3, 1809	"		By death, aged years.
90	Abigail (Marble) Beels (*Jacob)	"	"	Jan. 1, 1814	By death, aged years.
91	Rebecca (Safford) Caldwell (Nathan)	"	"	June 23, 1835	By death, aged 71 years.
92	Oliver Persons	Oct. 8, 1809	"	Oct. 4, 1821	Dis. to ch. in Weston.
93	Joshua Eaton	"	"	Oct. 21, 1821	Dis. to ch. in Adams, N. Y.
94	Rebecca (Kinney) Eaton (Joshua)	"	"		
95	Elisha Bisbee	"	"	Sept. 21, 1833	Exc. See Church Records.
96	Mary (Grout) Bisbee (Elisha)	"	"	July 5, 1862	By death, aged 78 years.
97	Anna (Pratt) Whitcomb (Jacob)	"	"	July 21, 1855	By death, aged 85 years.
98	Jerusha (Kenney) Field (Oliver)	"	"	Jan. 1, 1844	Dis. to ch. in Elk Grove, Ill.
99	David Boynton (Rev.)	Oct. 15, 1809	"	July 14, 1853	By death, aged 82 years.
100	Lydia (Nourse) Boynton (Rev. David)	"	"	Jan. 17, 1821	Dis. to ch. in Rockingham.
101	Calvin Hubbard	Oct. 29, 1809	"	Oct. 21, 1839	Dis. to ch. in Guildhall.
102	Anna (Meacham) Hubbard (Calvin)	"	"		"
103	Martha (Prentiss) Cobb (Dr. Moses)	Dec. 17, 1809	"	June 22, 1845	Dis. to Con. ch. Kalamazoo, Mich
104	Walter R. Gilkey (Dea.)	"	"	Jan. 4, 1829	Dis. to ch. in Middlebury.
105	Ebenezer Washburn (Rev.)	Jan. 7, 1810	"		By death, aged 77 years.
106	Mary (Lockwood) Chilson (Daniel)	Feb. 11, 1810	"	April 14, 1841	Dis. to ch. in Weathersfield.

No. & Name	Date	Profession of Faith	Date	Remarks
107 Hannah (Walter) Lynde (Elliot)	Feb. 11, 1810	"	Oct. 1, 1812	Dis. to ch. in Antwerp, N. Y.
108 Martha (Chamberlain) Nourse (Peter)	Feb. 18, 1810	"	Jan. 1, 1830	Dis. to ch. in Charlestown, N. H.
109 Sarah (White) Wheeler (Artemas)	March 10, 1810	"		Dis. to ch. in
110 Clarissa (Washburn) Hardy (Samuel)	"	"		Dis. to ch. in Chester.
111 Ann (Cobb) Jones (Charles)	"	"	Jan. 4, 1839	Dis. to ch. in Claremont, N. H.
112 Ann (Hubbard) Cleaveland (Jedediah)	"	"		Dis. to ch. in Guildhall
113 Eunice Pease	"	"		Dis. to ch. in Weathersfield
114 Sophia (Upham) Miller ( )	"	"	Aug. 4, 1832	By death, aged 46 years.
115 Experience (Stafford) Burge (Osman)	"	"	Sept. 2, 1837	By death, aged 61 years.
116 Susanna (Oakes) Whitney (Dea. Elijah)	"	"	July 25, 1854	By death, aged 61 years.
117 Clementine (Shattuck) Merrit (David M.)	"	"	Dec. 27, 1852	By death, aged 61 years.
118 Rosetta M. (Earle) Thornton (Salmon)	"	"		
119 Daniel Pratt	"	"	Sept. 27, 1849	By death, aged 77 years.
120 Jeduthan Cobb	"	"	March 7, 1830	Dis. to ch. in Westport, N. Y.
121 Weston Shattuck	"	"	Nov. 6, 1836	Dis. to ch. in Essex, N. Y.
122 Hartwell Shattuck	"	"		Dis. to ch. in Crown Point, N. Y.
123 Horace Hubbard	"	"	Oct. 21, 1839	Dis. to ch. in Guildhall.
124 Mary G. (Holden) Edgell (Moses)	March 29, 1810	"	June 22 1821	By death, aged 39 years.
125 Ebenezer Washburn	April 19, 1810	"	Sept. 3, 1829	Exc. See Church Records.
126 Abigail ( ) Washburn (Ebenezer)	"	"	Oct. 10, 1839	Dis. to ch. in Blendon, O.
127 Eleanor (Powers) Place (Warden)	May 5, 1810	Letter from ch. in Fisherfield, N.H.	Aug. 4, 1832	Dis. to ch. in Keeseville, N. Y.
128 Sarah ( ) Brown (&William)	May 7, 1810	Letter from ch. in Royalston, Ms.	May 3, 1839	Exc. See Church Records.
129 Catharine (Felch) Haywood (Dea. David)	Aug. 20, 1810	Profession of Faith.	July 2 1815	Dis. to ch. in Weathersfield.
130 Joseph Selden (Dea.)	"	"	Dec. 22, 1855	By death, aged 82 years.
131 Huldah (Bates) Selden (Dea. Joseph)	"	"	Nov. 15, 1849	By death, aged 72 years.
132 Nancy Bishee	"	"	July 11, 1830	Dis. to ch. in Waitsfield.
133 Hannah (Clark) Hatch (*)	Sept. 2, 1810	"		Dis. to ch. in
134 Polly (Newton) Woodward (Sam. Jr.)	"	"	Jan. 24, 1862	By death, aged 75 years.
135 Martha (Manning) Walker (Eph.)	Sept. 1 1811	"	March 1, 1835	By death, aged 63 years.
136 Parkman Davis	March 8, 1812	"	Jan. 16, 1836	By death, aged 63 years.
137 Sally (Forbush) Davis (Parkman)	March 9, 1812	"	April 10, 1864	By death, aged 87 years.
138 Eli Meade	May 3 1812	"	July 13, 1835	By death, aged 81 years.
139 Sarah ( ) Meade (Eli)	"	"		By death, aged years.
140 Elizabeth (Meade) Oakes (David)	"	"	Oct. 15, 1842	By death, aged 66 years.
141 Huldah (Stoddard) Bates (Roger)	"	"	Dec. 1, 1835	By death, aged 70 years.
142 Eunice (Nichols) Underwood (James)	"	"	Dec. 5, 1828	By death, aged 72 years.
143 Eve (Taylor) Clark (Abraham)	"	"	Feb. 27, 1820	Dis. to ch. in Crown Point, N.Y.
144 Mercy (Saford) Shattuck (Hartwell)	"	"		
145 Arethusa F. (Holden) Davis (Darius)	July 5, 1812	"	1835	Dis. to ch. in Saratoga, N. Y.
146 William Davis (Den.)	"	"	Sept. 15, 1858	By death, aged 79 years.
147 Phebe (Sanders) Davis (Den. Wm.)	"	"	Jan. 27, 1840	By death, aged 66 years.
148 Orathy (Selden) Fisher (Joseph)	"	"	Dec. 1, 1831	Dis. to ch. in Chester.

20

No.	Name	Date of Recept'n.	Manner of Reception.	Date of Removal.	Manner of Removal.
149	Sarah Burnham (Baltimore)	Aug. 2, 1812	Profession of Faith.		By death, aged years.
150	Molly (Gannet) Chamberlain (Isaac)	Aug. 16, 1812	"	July 3, 1814	Dis. to ch in Weathersfield.
151	Lydia (Whipple) Heald (Col. Amos)	Oct. 11, 1812	"	Oct. 15, 1821	Dis. to ch. in Chester.
152	Joseph Reed	Sept. 3, 1813,	"	Dec. 1, 1831	
153	Mary (Muzzy) Reed (Joseph)		"	May 2, 1817	Dis. to Bap. ch. in Chester.
154	Leafy R. Reed		"		By death, aged years.
155	Lois (Scollay) Stocker) (Elijah) Town (Aaron)		"		By death, aged years.
156	Lydia (Proctor) Shedd (Zach.)		"	June 1, 1848	By death, aged years.
157	Peter Nourse		Letter from ch. in Jaffrey, N. H.	Aug. 10, 1819	Dis. to ch. in Rockingham.
158	Martha ( ) Nourse (Peter)	May 1, 1814	Profession of Faith.		
159	Sophia (Holden) Steele (Samuel)	June 19, 1814	"	May 20, 1839	Dis. to ch. in Weathersfield E.
160	John Heald		"	Sept. 12, 1824	Dis. to ch. in Chester.
161	Esther (Smith) Heald (John)		"	"	
162	Betsey (Mather) Shattuck (Weston)	July 3, 1814	"	Nov. 6, 1836	Dis. to ch. in Essex, N. Y.
163	Elizabeth (Bisbee) Tolles (L) (Conant) (Ruf,) Tower (I)		"	July 15, 1828	By death, aged 52 years.
164	Thankful (Bates) Gill (Maj. John)		"		By death, aged years.
165	Phila Evans	Oct. 6, 1814	"		By death, aged 69 years.
166	Rhoda (Field) Haskins (Dr. Calvin)		"	Jan. 4, 1835	Dis. to ch. in Reading, Ms.
167	Lydia Mather		"		By death, aged years.
168	Jonathan Woodbury	Jan. 29, 1815	"	Sept. 4, 1842	By death, aged 75 years.
169	Sally (Davis) Woodbury (Jona.)		"	Jan. 31, 1851	By death, aged 76 years.
170	Horatio Gates Hawkins (Dea.)	Oct. 8, 1815	"	Oct. 16, 1826	Dis. to ch. in Manchester.
171	Polly (Bates) Hawkins (Dea. H. G.)		"		
172	Elizabeth Shedd		"		By death, aged 25 years.
173	Moses Fairbanks (Col.)	Jan. 3, 1816	"	March 15, 1821	Exc. See Church Records.
174	Jane (Priest) Russ (James)	May 2, 1816	"	June 14, 1834	
175	Fanny (Lathe) Conant (Rufus)	July 7 1816	"	July 1 1820	Dis. to ch. in Poultney.
176	Shubael Whitcomb	Oct. 12, 1816	Letter from ch. in Groton, Ms.	March 30, 1848	By death, aged 77 years.
177	Ruth (Lincoln) Whitcomb (Shubael)		Profession of Faith	July 9, 1864	By death, aged 87 years.
178	Polly (Wetherbee) Copeland (Smith)	Oct. 27, 1816	"	July 1, 1820	Dis. to ch in Antwerp, N. Y.
179	Nathaniel Caldwell	Nov. 21, 1816	Letter from ch. in N. Hampton, Ms	March 17, 1828	By death, aged 31 years.
180	John White	April 29, 1817	Profession of Faith.	May 4, 1826	By death, aged 60 years.
181	Elizabeth (Byington) Shedd (*Solomon)	May 5, 1817	Letter from ch. in Boylston, Ms.	May 4, 1820	By death, aged 80 years.
182	Nancy (Nichols) (Seymour) (David) Oakes (David)	Aug. 28 1817	Profession of Faith.	Nov. 24, 1822	Dis. to ch. in Ogdensburgh, N. Y.
183	Daniel Bourne	Oct. 17, 1819	"	Aug. 28, 1825	By death, aged 39 years.
184	Abigail (Gannet) Bourne (Daniel)		"	Oct. 19, 1863	By death, aged 72 years.
185	Anna Burge		"	Oct. 1, 1821	By death, aged 26 years.
186	Sarah (Tolles) Nichols (Amos)		Letter from ch. Ticonderoga, N. Y.	Dec. 1, 1831	Dis. to ch. in

No.	Name	Admitted	Mode	Removed	Disposition
187	Sarah (Smiley) Belknap (Josiah)	July 2, 1820	Letter from ch. in Jaffrey, N. H.	Feb. 20, 1846	By death, aged 82 years.
188	Achsah (White) Washburn (George)	"	Profession of Faith.	March 8, 1869	By death, aged 79 years.
189	Sarah (Gill) Putnam (Abraham)	Oct. 1, 1820	"	July 25, 1824	By death, aged 28 years.
190	Phinetta (Smith) Leach (Henry)	Oct. 26, 1820	"	Feb. 26, 1821	Dis. to ch. in T. Sem. Andover, Ms
191	Mary (Durrent) Hayden (Josiah)	May 8, 1821	Letter from ch. in Claremont, N.H.	Dec. 11, 1825	Dis. to ch. in Woodstock.
192	Seneca White (Rev.)	"	Profession of Faith.		"
193	Jacob Fisher	June 17, 1821	"	Oct. 11, 1836	Dis. to ch. in Felicity, O.
194	Clarissa (Johnson) Fisher (Jacob)	"	"	Jan. 1, 1864	By death, aged 70 years.
195	Mary Ann (Grimes) Stevens (Silsby)	"	"		Dis. to ch. in
196	Funny (Nichols) Stevens (Maj. John)	"	"		Dis. to ch. in
197	Dolly (Bixby) Cook (Ebenezer)	"	"		Dis. to ch. in
198	Abigail Bixby	"	"	July 11, 1836	Dis. to ch. in Whitefield.
199	Charlotte (Bixby) Taylor (Reuben)	"	"	July 1, 1853	Dis. to ch. in Roxbury, Ms.
200	Nancy (Nichols) Bowman (Thaddeus)	June 17, 1821	"	Sept. 1, 1829	Dis. to ch. in Sudbury, Ms.
201	Nancy (Bixbee) Randall (George)	"	"	Nov. 15, 1834	By death, aged 76 years.
202	Ruth (Whitman) Bates (Gibson)	"	"	Jan. 4, 1839	Dis. to ch. in Y. C., N. Haven, Ct.
203	Risqua B. (Newton) Pierce (William	"	"	April 27, 1848	Exc. See Church Records.
204	John Bislee	"	"	Sept. 12, 1824	Dis. to ch. in Guildhall.
205	James Bates Thomson	July 1, 1821	"	July 6, 1823	Dis. to ch. in Stoddard, N. H.
206	Moses Bixby	"	"	Aug. 1, 1823	Dis. to ch. in Chester.
207	Lemuel S. Hubbard	"	"	July 2, 1823	By death, aged 31 years.
208	Abram Whitman	"	"	July 1, 1831	Dis. to ch. in Wardsboro.
209	Hannah (Lewis) Clapp (Stephen)	"	Letter from ch. in Royalston, Ms.	March 20, 1827	By death, aged 70 years.
210	Jemima (French) Onion (Ichabod)	"	Profession of Faith.	May 15, 1836	Dis. to ch. in Athens.
211	Abigail ( ) (Amos (*	Sept. 16, 1821	"	Feb. 15, 1827	Dis.to 3d Pres.ch.in Allany, N.Y.
212	Joseph Bigelow White (Rev.)	Sept. 30, 1821	"	July 27, 1838	Dis. to ch. in Claremont, N.H.
213	Mary (Trask) Cutter (*William)	"	"	June 28, 1827	Dis. to ch. in Lyndon.
214	Martha (Bates) Whipple (Joel)	"	"	April 24, 1855	By death, aged 49 years.
215	Roxana Haskell	"	"	Nov. 6, 1831	Exc. See Church Records.
216	Content Haskell	"	"	June 18, 1837	By death, aged 67 years.
217	Ruth (Steele) Pierce (Joseph)	"	"	June 22, 1844	Dis.to Pres.ch.in Redford, Mich.
218	Edna (Steele) Tenney (Rev. S. G.)	"	"	June 23, 1833	Dis. to ch. in Hartford, Ct.
219	Helenry Steele	"	"	March 4, 1830	By death, aged 72 years.
220	Nonfas Cobb (Dea.)	Aug. 4, 1822	"	Nov. 6, 1842	By death, aged 36 years.
221	Ludowick Darrow	"	"		Exc. See Church Records.
222	Elijah Whitney (Dea.)	"	"		Dis. to ch. in Weathersfield E.
223	Joseph Selden Jr.	"	"		
224	John Meeks	"	"		
225	Peter White	"	"		
226	Ephraim Rogers	"	"		
227	Luke Scofield	"	"		
228	Ashbel Steele (Dea.) (933)	"	"		

No.	Name.	Date of Recep'n.	Manner of Reception.	Date of Removal.	Manner of Removal.
229	Ann Steele	Aug. 4, 1822	Profession of Faith.	March 10, 1849	By death, aged 54 years.
230	Hannah (Steele)(Powers)(Geo.) Davidson(Dea. Wm.)	"	"	Oct. 1, 1855	Dis. to 1st ch. in Lowell, Ms.
231	Harriet (Steele) Wise (Martin)	"	"	Feb. 3, 1839	Dis. to ch. in Cambridge.
232	Mary (Shafter) Lovell (Don)	"	"	July 31, 1842	Dis. to ch. in Ionia, Mich.
233	Betsey (Davis) Dana (Thomas)	"	"	Dec. 17, 1851	By death, aged 72 years.
234	Phebe (Pierce) Abbott (Israel)	"	"	July 31, 1835	Dis. to ch. in Charlestown, N.H.
235	Mary (House) Caldwell (Nathan)	"	"		
236	Cathee're (Davis) Whitcomb (Ezekiel)	"	"	Jan. 20, 1026	By death, aged 31 years.
237	Mary (Davis) Brown (John)	"	"		By death, aged years.
238	Sarah (Bowker) Proctor (Nathan)	"	"		Dis. to ch. in Chester.
239	Susan (Bradley) (Stoughton) (Thos.) Lane (Horace)	"	"	July 5, 1835	By death, aged 54 years.
240	Elsa Olney	"	"	March 26, 1855	By death, aged years.
241	Fanny (Glazier) Wool (Henry)	"	"	March 1, 1843	By death, aged 50 years.
242	Sally (Tower) Cook (Philip)	"	"	Aug. 18, 1639	
243	Threda (Tower) Gill (Daniel A.)	"	"		
244	Louis (Bates)(Rogers)(Eph)(Burge)(O)Hawkins(HG)	"	"	Nov. 6, 1831	Dis. to ch. in Redford, Mich.
245	Olive (Whitcomb) Selden (Joseph Jr.)	"	"	May 22, 1834	Exc. See Church Records.
246	Betsey (Bisbee) Parks (Jefferson)	"	"	July 31, 1834	Dis. to ch. in Charlestown, Ms.
247	Anna (Hildreth) Hildreth (Samuel)	"	"	March 5, 1843	Dis. to ch. in Chesterfield, N.H
248	Sarah (Randall) Leete (Jeremiah)	"	"	April 23, 1855	By death, aged 64 years.
249	Meriel (Bates) Cobb (Dea. Nomlas)	"	"	July 22, 1833	Dis. to ch. in Guildhall.
250	Harriet (Washburn) Washburn (Zeph. K.)	"	"	Oct. 30, 1831	Dis. to ch. in Chester.
251	Mary (Oakes) Lovell (James)	"	"	April 8, 1838	By death, aged 68 years.
252	Elizabeth (Rogers) Rogers (Jona)	"	"	Oct. 16, 1836	Dis. to ch. in Manchester.
253	Mary (Hawkins) Barnard (George)	"	"	March 8, 1837	By death, aged 25 years.
254	Elizabeth (Smiley) Williams (Henry)	"	"	1831	Dis. to ch. in Redford, Mich.
255	Allen Bates (601)	Oct. 13, 1822	"		"
256	Anna (Bates) Bates (Allen) (602)	"	"		
257	Silence Mann	"	"	Nov. 21, 1825	Dis. to ch. in Chester.
258	Pamelia (Hubbard) Nichols (Hiram H.)	"	"	Jan. 4, 1839	Dis. to ch. in Guildhall.
259	Sally Perry	March 16, 1823	"		By death, aged years.
260	Nancy (Oakes) Lewis (Samuel M.)	"	"	Dec. 22, 1833	By death, aged 52 years.
261	Amanda (Grimes) Davis (James)	"	"	April 17, 1865	By death, aged 59 years.
262	John Stevens 2d	"	"	Oct. 11, 1835	Dis. to ch. in Felicity, O.
263	Lydia (Bragg) Robinson (Elijah)	May 11, 1823	"	March 14, 1820	Dis. to ch. in Moretown.
264	Nancy (Tower) Safford (Noah)	"	"	Aug. 10, 1854	By death, aged 66 years.
265	Rachel (Tower) Bates (Davis)	"	"	May 1, 1827	Dis. to ch. in Chester. (942)
266	Lucy (Durrent) Locke (Daniel'	May 30, 1823			

No.	Name	Admitted	Manner	Date	Remarks
267	Sally [Cutler] Holman [Chauncey]	June 29, 1823	Profession of Faith.	Sept. 21, 1829	By death, aged 61 years,
268	Susanna [Leland] Durrant [Luther]	"	"	Jan. 20, 1836	Dis. to ch. in Waitsfield.
269	Ruth [Adams] Smith [Joseph]	"	"	Nov. 2, 1840	By death, aged 74 years.
270	Mary Darling	July 4, 1824	"	Jan. 1, 1833	Dis. to ch. in Charlottesville, Va.
271	Eli Ames	"	"	"	Dis. to ch. in Charlottesville, Va.
272	Nancy [Organ] Ames [Eli]	Sept. 5, 1824	"		Dis. to ch. in Charlottesville, Va.
273	Nancy Ann Clark	Oct. 10, 1824	"	Nov. 2, 1833	Dis. to ch. in
274	Sally [Belknap] Powers [William]	July 3, 1825	"	April 30, 1836	Exc. See Church Records.
275	Susanna Smith [Selden] Jewett [Rev. S.]	Aug. 7, 1825	Letter from ch. in Fitchburg, Ma.	Sept. 7, 1825	Dis. to ch. in Evansville. Ill.
276	Nancy House	Sept. 1, 1825	Profession of Faith.	Feb. 1, 1833	By death, aged 30 years.
277	Perrin N. Richards	"	"	"	Dis. to ch. in Townsend, Ms.
278	Emily [ ] Richards Perrin N.	"	"		"
279	Sarah Proctor	"	"		Dis. to ch. in
280	Jane Powell	"	"		Dis. to ch. in Troy.
281	Ray Davis	July 1, 1827	Letter from ch. in Portland, Me.	Sept. 26, 1833	Exc. See Church Records.
282	Mercy Harris	"	Letter from ch. in	Sept. 20, 1839	By death, aged 57 years.
283	Osman Burge	"	Letter from ch. in Weathersfield.	Aug. 23, 1848	By death, aged 59 years.
284	Isaac M. Lewis [Dea.]	"	Letter from ch. in Ballston, N.Y.	Nov. 29, 1846	Dis. to ch. in Bronson, Mich.
285	John Jennison Barnard (994)	"	Letter from ch. in Lebanon, N.H.	May 15, 1826	Exc. See Church Records.
286	Priscilla [Hodgkins] Brown [Abel]	"	Letter from ch. in Acworth, N.H.	March 31, 1837	By death, aged years.
287	Eunice [ ] Litchfield [Hersey]	"	"	Sept. 2, 1837	
288	Elizabeth Barrett	July 10, 1829	"		
289	Nancy [Campbell] Wilkins [Alvah]	June 10, 1829	Profession of Faith.	Sept. 1, 1833	Dis. to ch. in
290	Lydia [Bowns] [Spalding] [Danl.] Belknap [Lewis]	"	"	Feb. 1, 1830	By death, aged 25 years.
291	Nancy B. Goodman [Rev. E. W.]	July 1, 1829.	"	March 15, 1830	By death, aged 30 years.
292	Mary Barrett	Jan. 1, 1831	"	March 24, 1850	By death, aged 74 years.
293	John Davidson	"	"	April 10, 1859	By death, aged 80 years.
294	Abigail [Prouty] Davidson [John]	"	"		
295	Frederic Parks	"	"		
296	Arba Holman [Dea.]	"	Profession of Faith.	Feb. 20, 1864	Dis. to ch. in Windham.
297	Hannah [Clark] Holman [Dea. A.]	"	"		
298	Calvin Selden [Rev.]	"	"		
299	Theophilus Bates	"	"	Jan. 28, 1847	By death, aged 84 years.
300	Parkman Davis Jr.	"	"	Sept. 4, 1840	Dis. to Bap. ch. in N. Springfield.
301	Chauncey Davis	"	"		
302	Tural R. Davis	"	"	Nov. 2, 1838	Dis. to ch. in Chester.
303	Delight B. [Damon] [Cutler] [L.] Whitcomb [Peroz]	March 1, 1831	"		
304	Nancy [Anthony] Cushing [Daniel] (766)	Nov. 6, 1831	"	Nov. 16, 1837	Dis. to ch. in Quechee.
305	Fanny [Leland] Hayden [J.] Dyer [Wm.]	"	"	Oct. 2, 1836	Dis. to Bap. ch. in N. Springfield.
306	Irene [Davis] Webster [Albert A.]	"	"	Feb. 18, 1844	Dis. to ch. in Irasburg.
307	Mary Davis	"	"	March 17, 1840	By death, aged 28 years.
308	Wells Harlow	"	"	March 17, 1847	Exc. See Church Records.

24

No.	Name.	Date of Recept'n.	Manner of Reception.	Date of Removal.	Manner of Removal.
309	Adeline Stevens	Nov. 6, 1831	Profession of Faith.	Oct. 25, 1835	Dis to ch. in Felicity, O.
310	Mary A. Colburn	"	"	April 30, 1858	Exc. See Church Records.
311	Alexander H. Johnson	"	"	July 5, 1834	Exc. See Church Records.
312	John B. Bisbee	"	"	March 20, 1836	Dis. to ch. in Waitsfield.
313	Sally [Merriam] Whipple [James]	"	"	Aug. 9, 1846	By death, aged 78 years.
314	Lucretia [Brown] Whitcomb [Israel]	"	"	June 17, 1869	By death, aged 59 years.
315	Asahel Putnam	"	"	July 31, 1835	Dis. to ch. in Charlestown, N. H.
316	Abraham J. Bourne [Dea.]	"	"	June 11, 1848	Dis. to Pine St. ch. in Boston, Ms.
317	Nancy [Barrett] Smiley [Harkness]	"	"	July 1, 1854	Dis. to ch. in Knoxville, Tenn.
318	Betsey [Davis] Montague [Stephen]	"	"	Oct. 24, 1837	Dis. to ch. in Chelsea.
319	William Dodge	"	"	Nov. 3, 1837	Dis. to ch. in
320	Abigail [Garfield] Dodge [William]	"	"	"	Dis. to ch. in
321	Theoda [Russell] Durrent [Joseph Jr.]	"	"	Aug. 14, 1835	Dis. to ch. in Poultney.
322	Sybil [Bates] Whipple [Ormus M.]	"	"		
323	Zilpha [Spalding] Nourse [Hiram]	"	"	Nov. 20, 1864	By death, aged 64 years.
324	Sabrina [Brush] Whipple [James]	"	"	Nov. 15, 1844	Exc. See Church Records.
325	Eliza [Williams] Burke [Russell]	"	"		
326	Lucy Maria [Barnard] Steele [Dea. A.] (934)	"	"	Nov. 6, 1842	Dis. to ch. in Weathersfield E.
327	Mary Ann Ellison	"	"	July 1, 1840	Dis. to ch. in
328	Mary Ruth [Pratt] Whitney [Norman K.]	"	"	May 3, 1835	Dis. to ch. in West Rutland.
329	Jane [Pratt] Hyde [Henry]	"	"		Dis. to ch. in Lynn, Ms.
330	Phebe [Eggleston] Page [Abel]	"	Letter from ch. in Essex, N. Y.		
331	Hannah [Thayer] Porter [Fred A.]	"	Profession of Faith.		
332	Elizabeth Woodbury	"	"	Feb. 4, 1836	Dis. to ch. in Perkinsville.
333	Maria [Woodbury] Lewis [Daniel]	"	"		
334	Betsey [Bates] Johnson [George]	"	"		
335	Emily Ridgeway	"	"	1832	Dis. to ch. in Roxbury, Ms.
336	Hannah Prentiss	"	"		
337	Polly Whitcomb	"	"	March 29, 1841	By death, aged 41 years.
338	Betsey [Whitcomb] Woodbury [Daniel]	"	"	Jan. 20, 1836	Dis. to ch. in Perkinsville.
339	Esther [Bates] Tower [Stoddard]	"	"	Oct. 3, 1851	By death, aged 39 years.
340	Elizabeth [Bourne] Woodbury [Dea. Joel]	"	"	Dec. 14, 1864	By death, aged 48 years.
341	Sarah [Foster] Crain [Eleazer]	"	"	Aug. 19, 1839	By death, aged 49 years.
342	Anna [Closson] Floyd [Henry]	"	"	July 5, 1839	Dis. to ch. in Westminster E.
343	Sally [Bates] Tower [Stoddard]	"	"	Oct. 28, 1839	By death, aged 45 years.
344	Eunice Williams	"	"		
345	Arethusa Bisbee	"	"		
346	Mary [Bisbee] Bailey [Erastus B.]	"	"	July 11, 1835	Dis. to ch. in Waitsfield. "

No. & Name	Admitted	Manner	Date	Remarks
347 Sarah [Burge] Burgess [Sylvanus]	Nov. 6, 1831	Profession of Faith.	July 9, 1837	Dis. to ch. in Grafton.
348 Louisa [Chipman] [Hotchkiss [Elson] Jones [Don.]	Jan. 1, 1832	"	1846	Dis. to ch. in Putney.
349 Horatio Bates Hawkins	"	"	Aug. 23, 1835	Dis. to ch. in Manchester.
350 Abigail [dale] Hawkins [Horatio B.]	"	"		
351 Israel Whitcomb	Jan. 8, 1832	"	Sept. 23, 1849	Dis. to Pres. ch. in Alton, Ill.
352 Sarah Jane [Smiley] Sawyer [Seth]	"	"	Sept. 19, 1866	By death, aged 64 years.
353 Lydia Caldwell	"	"	Oct. 1, 1841	Dis. to ch. in Chester.
354 Lucretia O. [Whitney] Lovell [James] (919)	"	"		
355 Rebecca [Rice] Graham [Dana]	"	"	Oct. 24, 1865	By death, aged 52 years.
356 Henry Prentiss Jr.	March 1, 1832	"	March 25, 1851	Dis. to ch. in Portland, Oregon.
357 Nancy [Bates] Atkinson [Rev. G. H.]	April 2, 1832	"	April 10, 1832	By death, aged 95 years.
358 Mary Corlew	April 9, 1832	"	Jan. 20, 1836	Dis. to ch. in Waitsfield.
359 Luther Durrent	Aug. 4, 1832	"	Feb. 1, 1856	Dis. to ch. in Winchendon, Ms.
360 Daniel O. Morton [Rev.]	"	"	"	"
361 Lucretia [Parsons] Morton [Rev. D. O.]		Letter from ch. in Shoreham.		
362 Electa F. [Morton] Minot [Jonas]				
363 Sarah [ ] Brown [William]	Sept. 2, 1832	Letter from ch. in Mt. Holly.	Jan. 6, 1840	By death, aged 70 years.
364 Hannah [Ames] Cummings [Daniel]	"	Letter from ch. in Andover, Ms.	Feb. 6, 1837	Dis. to ch. in Haverhill, Ms.
365 Hannah [Cummings] Williams [Luke]	"		Jan. 21, 1835	By death, aged 30 years.
366 Almira Louisa Walker	"	Profession of Faith	July 27, 1841	By death, aged 40 years.
367 Lydia [Litchfield] Hurd [Harvey]	"	"	June 11, 1843	Dis. to ch. in Surry, N. H.
368 Daniel Griswold	Nov. 4, 1832	"	Aug. 4, 1836	By death, aged 74 years.
369 Joseph Durrent	"	"	Aug. 14, 1835	Dis. to ch. in Pontney.
370 Sarah [Gilson] Durrent [Jos.]	"	"		
371 Welcome Olney	"	"		Exc. See Church Records.
372 Calvin Durrent (543)	"	"	Sept. 6, 1834	Dis. to M. E. ch. in Springfield.
373 Smith Randall	"	"	Nov. 13, 1835	By death, aged 31 years.
374 Mary Walker	"	"	July 6, 1840	By death, aged 86 years.
375 William Bragg	"	"	Dec. 8, 1849	By death, aged 75 years.
376 Luke Brown	"	"	Sept. 1, 1857	
377 Abigail [Bates] Ellis [Jacob]	Jan. 13, 1833	"	Nov. 13, 1835	Dis. to M. E. ch. in Springfield.
378 Elvira [Davidson] Parks [Frederic]	March 3, 1833	"	July 8, 1838	Dis. to ch. in Burlington.
379 Betsey [Messenger] Martin [Jona.]	"	"		
380 Oscar Brown	"	"	Oct. 16, 1836	Dis. to ch. in Manchester.
381 Martha [Hawkins] Brown [Oscar]	"	"		
382 Christina [Hawkins] Swift [Theodore]	"	"		
383 Persis H. [Hawkins] Underhill [H.]	"	"	June 25, 1837	Dis. to ch. in Troy.
384 Stephen Blanchard	"	"		
385 Rebecca [Dutton] Blanchard [Stephen]	"	Letter from ch. in Troy.		
386 Louisa Pierce	April 24, 1833	Profession of Faith.	April 6, 1839	Dis. to ch. in Weathersfield E.
387 Statira [Booth] Miller [John]	May 6, 1833	Letter from ch. in Lempster, N. Y.	Feb. 25, 1844	By death, aged years.
388 Priscilla E. [West] [Burnham] [L.] Walker [Cephas]	"	Profession of Faith.	April 6, 1839	Dis. to ch. in Weathersfield E.
389 Lucy G. [Brown] Pingry [Judge W. M.]	"	"	Aug. 25, 1837	Dis. to Bap. ch. in Waitsfield.

No.	Name.	Date of Recept'n.	Manner of Reception.	Date of Removal.	Manner of Removal.
390	Nathaniel Pierce	May 6, 1833	Profession of Faith.	April 6, 1839	Dis. to ch. in Weathersfield E.
391	Anna [Woolbury] Pierce [Nathaniel]	"	"	"	"
392	Susannah [Westcott] Streeter [Obadiah]	"	"	June 1856	By death, aged 64 years.
393	George Barnard	"	"	Oct. 16, 1836	Dis to ch. in Manchester.
394	Jacob Whitcomb	"	"	June 8, 1844	By death, aged 79 years.
395	Salmon Whitcomb [Salmon]	"	"	April 19, 1840	Dis. to ch. in Keene, N. H.
396	Fanny [Selden] Whitcomb [Salmon]				
397	James Davidson			Nov. 15, 1844	Exc. See Church Records.
398	Elmira [Webber] Mason [William]	May 19, 1833	Letter f. Bap. ch. in Acworth, N.H.	Oct. 30, 1864	By death, aged 76 years.
399	Eunice [Crawford] Wales [*Aaron]	June 15, 1833	Letter from ch. in Lowell, Ms.	April 6, 1839	Dis. to ch. in Weathersfield E.
400	Lydia [Reed] West [John]	June 21, 1833	Profession of Faith.	Feb. 25, 1847	Dis. to ch. in Claremont, N. H.
401	Ruth [Cobb] Hubbard [Isaac]	June 22, 1833	Letter from ch. in Claremont,N.H.	Nov. 16, 1837	Dis. to ch. in Quechee.
402	Zerviah [Chamlin] Cushing [Daniel]	July 7, 1833	Profession of Faith.	Sept. 30, 1839	By death, aged 83 years.
403	Jonathan Rogers			March 11, 1838	Dis. to ch. in Townshend.
404	Mary C. [Wilson] Wilkinson [Stephen R.]			Oct. 11, 1835	Dis. to ch. in Felicity, O.
405	Mary A. [Stevens] Tenney [Willard]			Jan. 20, 1836	Dis. to ch. in Waitsfield.
406	Martha M. Nourse [Peter U.]	Sept. 1, 1833 .		Sept. 17, 1837	Dis. to ch. in Waitsfield.
407	Nancy [Lockwood] Chipman [Samuel]	Nov. 3, 1833		Jan. 25, 1839	Dis. to ch. in Westminister E.
408	Laura Chipman			May 11, 1834	By death, aged 28 years.
409	Eliza Ann [White] Spencer [Jonas B.]			April 5, 1839	Dis. to ch. in Weathersfield E.
410	Abigail [Pierce] Spencer [Solomon]			July 3, 1842	Dis to ch. in Ionia, Mich.
411	Mary S. [Lovell] Hodges [Samuel]			Sept. 7, 1836	Dis. to ch. in Newport, N. H.
412	Grace [Mellors] Burke [Elijah]			Oct. 1, 1841	Dis. to ch. in Quincy, Ms.
413	Submit D. [ ] Holden [John]	March 2, 1834	Letter from ch. in Groton, Ms.		
414	Joseph Smith	July 6, 1834	Letter f. M. E. ch. in Rockingham.		
415	Sarah [Fletcher] Kenney [Daniel]		Letter from Bap. ch. in Chester.	Aug. 27, 1859	By death, aged 52 years.
416	Lucinda Works		Profession of Faith.		
417	Willard Tenney	Sept. 7, 1834	Letter from ch. in W. Brattleboro.	Oct. 11 1835	Dis. to ch. in Felicity, O.
418	Abby Day	"	Letter from ch. in Hartford, Ct.	July 12, 1838	By death, aged 22 years.
419	Susannah [Thayer] Brown [David]	"	Profession of Faith.	July 17, 1857	By death, aged 65 years.
420	Sally Brown Thomson				
421	Leonard Harrington	Nov. 2, 1834		April 30, 1836	Exc. See Church Records.
422	Abigail [Bixley] Tyrell [Artemas]	"	"	June 27, 1852	Dis. to ch. in
423	Lucia [Hubbard] Keyes [Jotham]			Nov. 21, 1841	Dis. to ch. in Guildhall.
424	Hannah S. [ ] Coffin [ ]			Jan. 1, 1846	Dis. to ch. in Brooklyn N. Y.
425	Aaron L. Thompson	Nov. 23, 1834		Feb. 6, 1867	By death, aged 64 years.
426	Russell Burke	Nov. 23, 1834		Oct. 4, 1852	By death, aged 55 years.
427	Noah Safford			Nov. 18, 1863	By death, aged 74 years.

	Name	Profession of Faith		Remarks
428	Don Lovell	Nov. 23 1834		By death, aged 34 years.
429	Samuel Chipman	"	Sept. 17, 1837	Dis. to ch. in Waitsfield
430	Jacob Pomeroy	"	Nov. 15, 1844	Exc. See Church Records.
431	Seymour Lockwood	"		
432	Lucy (Allee) Lockwood (Seymour)	"		
433	Hamlin Whitmore	"	Jan. 20, 1830	Exc. See Church Records.
434	Abel Brown	"	April 30, 1830	Exc. See Church Records.
435	George D. Burgess (658)	"	June 3, 1835	Dis. to Pres. ch. in W. Union, O.
436	Simon Stevens	"	Oct. 11, 1835	Dis. to ch. in Felicity O.
437	Frederic Barnard	"	April 24, 1863	Dis to ch. in Sycamore, Ill.
438	Ira Davis	"		
439	George C. Powers	"	Nov. 1, 1850	Exc. See Church Records.
440	Moses Rush Cobb	"	Jan. 7, 1845	Exc. See Church Records.
441	Rollin Clark	"	Nov. 1, 1850	Exc. See Church Records.
442	Noah Cook Taylor	"		By death, aged years.
443	Mary Ann (French) Haywood (M. D.)	"		
444	Franklin Keyes	"	Oct. 18, 1844	Exc. See Church Records.
445	Enoch Lake	"	March 20, 1836	Dis. to ch. in Quincy Ms.
446	Charlotte (Brackett) Lake (Enoch)	"	"	"
447	John Chipman	"		
448	Gratia (Bates) Chipman (John)	"		
449	James Walker	"		
450	Mary (Bisbee) Walker (James)	"		
451	Isaac Tower	"	April 2, 1860	By death, aged 73 years.
452	Susanna (Field) Tower (Isaac)	"	April 24, 1849	By death, aged 60 years.
453	Daniel Cushing (765)	"	Nov. 6, 1850	By death, aged 65 years.
454	Frederic W. Burgess	"	Nov. 16, 1837	Dis. to ch. in Quechee.
455	Elijah Bisbee	"	Oct. 3, 1841	Dis. to ch. in Denmark, Iowa.
456	Jacob Ellis	"	Nov. 26, 1847	Exc. See Church Records.
457	Hiram H. Nichols	"	Sept. 5, 1853	By death, aged 59 years.
458	Pamelia (Hubbard) Nichols (Hiram H.)	"	Oct. 21, 1839	Dis. to ch. in Guildhall.
459	John Brooks	"	"	"
460	Lydia (Fisher) Brooks (John)	"	Nov. 2, 1839	Dis. to ch. in Chester
461	Ormus Mandell Whipple	"	"	"
462	Hiram Bisbee	"	Aug. 25, 1848	Exc. See Church Records.
463	Betsey (Campbell) Bisbee (Hiram)	"	April 5, 1835	Exc. See Church Records.
464	William Dodge	"	Oct. 1, 1860	By death, aged 59 years.
465	Fanny (Richards) Porter (Judge S. W.)	"		Dis. to ch. in
466	Daniel Smith	"	March 11, 1869	By death, aged 82 years.
467	Lucia (Pomeroy) Smith (Daniel)	"	Dec. 20, 1834	Dis. to ch. in Perkinsville.
468	Francis K. Nichols	"	"	"
469	Frances (Boynton) Nichols (Francis K.)	"	"	"
470	Bethiah (Field) Tower (Abraham)	"	Sept. 11, 1839	By death, aged 53 years.

No.	Name.	Date of Recept'n.	Manner of Reception.	Date of Removal.	Manner of Removal.
471	Lucy (Wood) Bellows (Daniel)	Nov. 23, 1834	Profession of Faith.	Jan. 7, 1836	Dis. to Mr. E. ch. in Springfield.
472	Belinda (Parker) Fling (Asa)	"	"	Aug. 1, 1835	Dis. to ch.in Charlestown,N. H.
473	Elizabeth S. (Tower) Johnson (Nelson A.)	"	"	June 7, 1844	By death, aged 38 years.
474	Merrill (Brown) Bancroft (George)	"	"	March 31, 1837	Exc. See Church Records.
475	Lucia (Brown) Parker (Leonard)	"	"	May 3, 1839	Exc. See Church Records.
476	Jane (Brown) Demary (Andrew J.)	"	"	March 12, 1847	Exc. See Church Records.
477	Harriet Putnam	"	"	Aug. 1, 1835	Dis. to ch.in Charlestown, N.H.
478	Cynthia Putnam	"	"	June 7, 1835	Dis. to ch. in Malden, Ms.
479	Lucretia P. (Morton) Safford (Myron W.)	"	"	Feb. 2, 1836	Dis. to ch. in Winchendon, Ms.
480	Harriet Wright	"	"		
481	Louisa (Williams) Hall (John)	"	"	July 5, 1867	Dis. to ch. in Chester.
482	Catharine (Burke) Pratt (Thomas W.)	"	"	June 11, 1848	Dis. to Pine St. ch. Boston, Ms.
483	Elizabeth (Cobb) Steele (Eleazer)	"	"	March 5, 1861	By death, aged 45 years.
484	Susan L. (Brown) Barnard (Fred N.)	"	"	Jan. 30, 1841	Dis. to ch. in Westminster E.
485	Nancy (Gill) Richardson (John C.)	"	"	Oct. 27, 1850	Dis. to ch. Grafton.
486	Sarah (Gill) Rice (Oscar)	"	"	July 23, 1839	Dis. to ch., Grafton.
487	Sally (Barrett) Pettingill (Dea. Jona S.)	"	"	March 17, 1864	Dis. to ch. in Feeding Hills, Ms.
488	Lydia (Bates) Grout (Rev. Lewis)	"	"	March 21, 1869	By death, aged 63 years.
489	Sarah (Kemary) Clark (George R.)	"	"	Dec. 1, 1857	By death, aged 77 years.
490	Mary (Poole) Davis (Joshua)	"	"		
491	Phebe (Davis) Whitcomb (Jairus)	"	"		
492	Mary Ann (Carley) Stevens (Silsby)	"	"	May 1, 1836	Dis. to ch. in Felicity, O.
493	Elvira (Litchfield) Lord (George)	"	"	Nov. 1, 1839	Dis. to M. E. ch. in Springfield.
494	Sarah (Whitcomb) Spencer (John H.)	"	"	Sept. 11, 1838	By death, aged 44 years.
495	Susannah Durrent	"	"		
496	Emeline S. Durrent	"	"	Jan. 20, 1836	Dis. to ch. in Waitsfield.
497	Polly Barnes	"	"	May 1, 1835	Dis. to ch. in Charlestown,N.H.
498	William E. Fling	"	"		
499	Sarah (Earl) Fling (William)	"	"		
500	Hubbard Cabot	"	"	Feb. 8, 1841	Dis. to Pres. ch. in Troy, N. Y.
501	James Chipman	"	"	Feb. 23, 1836	Dis. to ch. in Waitsfield.
502	Almira (Harlow) Chipman (James) (1120)	"	"		"
503	William Pierce	"2"	"	Jan. 2, 1836	Exc. See Church Records.
504	Peter U. Nonrae	"	"	Jan. 20, 1836	Dis. to ch. fn Waitsfield.
505	Jerusha Smith	"	"	Dec. 8 1839	By death, aged 25 years.
506	Sarah Woodward	"	"	June 29, 1837	Dis. to M. E. ch. in Woodstock
507	George Jenkins	"	"		
508	Morrill (Thomson) Jenkins (George)	"	"		

	Name	Profession of Faith.		
509	Susan (Pratt) Miller (John)	Nov. 23, 1834	Aug. 23, 1850	Dis. to ch. In Oregon, Wis.
510	Elizabeth (Pratt) Nash (George)	"	Dec. 1, 1850	Dis. to ch. in Lynn, Ms.
511	Caroline (White) Tower (Daniel)	"	Sept. 24, 1837	Dis. with general Letter.
512	Norman K. Whitney	"	March 3, 1837	Exc. See Church Records.
513	Edmund P. Anthony	"	Sept. 12, 1841	Dis. to ch. in No. Hadley, Ma.
514	Martha (Dyke) Tolles (Clark)	"	April 0, 1839	Dis. to ch. in Weathersfield E.
515	Christopher Dodge	"	April 30, 1858	Exc. See Church Records.
516	David House	"	May 1, 1836	Dis. to ch. in Felicity, O.
517	Jonas Bates Spencer	"	Jan. 8, 1846	Exc. See Church Records.
518	Isaac G. Davis			Dis. to ch. in Felicity, O.
519	Don A. Pomeroy	Nov. 30, 1834	July 15, 1838	By death, aged 74 years.
520	Lemmel Cutler	"	Oct. 22, 1837	Dis. to ch. in Haverhill, Ms.
521	Sarah Cummings	"	Nov. 13, 1840	Dis. to ch. in Bridport.
522	Mary (Bragg) Day (Calvin)	"	Oct. 13, 1839	Dis. to ch. in Salisbury, N. H.
523	Elizabeth (Day) Jones (Philander)	"	Nov. 13, 1835	Dis. to ch. in Chester.
524	Amasa Woolson (Dea.) (909)	"	Aug. 6, 1837	By death, aged 70 years.
525	Frederic A. Porter	"	March 17, 1867	Dis. to ch. in Rawsonville, O.
526	Abner A. Bisbee	"	May 28, 1869	Dis. to ch. in Rawsonville, O.
527	Martha A. (Warner) Bisbee (Abner A.)	"	May 1, 1836	Dis. to ch. in Felicity, O.
528	Silsby Stevens	"	Oct. 1, 1841	Dis. to ch. in Quincy, Ms.
529	John Holden	"	June 7, 1835	Dis. to ch in Castleton.
530	Timothy W. Rice	"		
531	Joseph Messer	"		
532	Mary (Stoddard) Messer (Joseph)	"	March 19, 1852	By death, aged 60 years.
533	Hannah (Lovell) Wood (Col. Boz.)	"		
534	Abner Bisbee	"		
535	Cynthia (Ralph) Bisbee (Abner)	"	Nov. 29, 1839	Exc. See ch. Records.
536	William Brown	"	April 5, 1867	Dis. to ch. in Peru.
537	Ann (Richardson) Thompson (Elisha S.)	"	March 21, 1835	Dis. to ch. in Charlestown, N.H.
538	Almora (Bonney) Conant (Dean)	"	Jan. 24, 1847	Dis. to ch. in Salisbury.
539	Ruth Hubbard	"	Dec. 22, 1847	By death, aged 32 years.
540	Sarah Johnson	"	Aug. 9, 1838	Dis. to ch. in Lincoln, Ill.
541	Harriet (Johnson)Cochrane(Dea. Samuel C.)	"		
542	Eliza Selden	"	Nov. 1, 1835	By death, aged 66 years.
543	Smith Holman	"		
544	Selden Cook	"		
545	Mary (Batchelder) Cook (Selden)	"	Sept. 5, 1841	Dis. to ch. in Barre, Ma.
546	Ellen M. (Whitcomb) Spencer (John H.)	"	April 6, 1835	Exc. See Church Records.
547	Dean Cobb	"	Aug. 5, 1854	By death, aged 39 years.
548	Mary Tower (Spencer) Aldrich (Sam.)	"	Nov. 27, 1836	Dis. to M. E. ch. in Springfield.
549	Solomon Johnson	"	Oct. 29, 1858	Exc. See Church Records.
550	William T. Bourne	"		By death, aged years.
551	Jesse Morse Smith	"		

No.	Name.	Date of Recept'n	Manner of Reception.	Date of Removal.	Manner of Removal.
552	Adeline (Johnson) Pierce (William)	Nov. 30, 1834.	Profession of Faith.	Jan. 12, 1838	Exc. See Church Records.
553	Sarah Hawkins	"	"	June 4, 1847	Dis. to Bap. ch. Brooklyn, N. Y.
554	Ann (Tolles) Stimpson (David)	"	"	May 1, 1848	By death, aged 79 years.
555	George Richardson Clark	"	"		
556	Sarah T. (Cook) Grinnell (Abel)	"	"	June 3, 1849	By death, aged 26 years.
557	Juliette (Selden) Chase (Austin P.)	"	"	Feb. 1, 1845	By death, aged 24 years.
558	Caroline M. Stevens	"	"	May 1, 1836	Dis. to ch. in Felicity, O.
559	Abigail (Ellis) Smith (Charles)	"	"	July 8, 1850	Dis. to Ep. ch. in Marion, O.
560	Sarah (Brown) Parker (Henry)	"	"	May 3, 1839	Exc. See Church Records.
561	Martha Jane Davis	"	"	Jan. 1, 1844	By death, aged 24 years.
562	Mary Blanchard	"	"	June 25, 1837	Dis. to ch. in Troy.
563	Abigail Johnson Lovell	"	"	July 31, 1842	Dis. to ch. in Ionia, Mich.
564	Martha Jane (Nourse) Haywood (Dea. G. P.)	"	"		
565	Ephraim Walker Jr.	"	"	Feb. 28, 1866	By death, aged 63 years
566	John Works	"	"	June 6, 1841	Dis. to ch. in Weston.
567	Charles L. Thayer	"	"	Dec. 12, 1854	Dis. to ch. in Perkinsville.
568	Mary Ann (Crawford) Thayer (Chas. L.)	"	"	"	"
569	Hyren Henry	"	"		
570	Artemas Deau	"	"		
571	Amelia (Smith) Spencer (Peter H.)	"	"	Aug. 27, 1843	Dis. to ch. in Claremont, N.H.
572	Rosabello Harrington	"	"	"	"
573	Nancy L. (Thornton) Tower (Abraham Jr.)	"	"	May 27, 1853	By death, aged 36 years.
574	Sally (Stocker) Snell (Martin)	"	"		
575	Sarah Tabitha (Perry) Works (John)	"	"	Jan. 6, 1841	Dis. to ch. in Weston.
576	Sarah Bates (Tower) Crombie (John G.)	"	"	Sept. 9, 1849	Dis. to ch. in Pontiac, Mich.
577	Cynthia Munsell	"	"	July 31, 1835	Dis. to ch. in Charlestown, N. H.
578	Marcia Maria Nourse	"	"	April 5, 1839	Dis. to ch. in Weathersfield E.
579	Lorinda (Pierce) Bowen (Maurice D.)	"	"	"	"
580	Mary (West) Jaseph (George W.)	Dec. 28, 1834	"		
581	Mary (Davidson) Woolson (Amasa) (Dea.)	"	"	Feb. 18, 1840	Dis. to ch. in Chester.
582	Mary Woodbury	"	"		
583	Lydia Davis	"	"		
584	Thomas M. Pratt	"	"	Jan. 1, 1846	Dis. to M. E. ch. Claremont, N.H.
585	John Greeley	"	"	July 5, 1867	Dis. to ch. in Chester.
586	Sophia (Bates) Pomeroy (Jacob)	"	"	Oct. 1, 1841	Dis. to ch. in Quincy, Ms.
587	Nancy (Williams) Locke (Dea. O.)	Jan. 25, 1835	Letter from ch. in Cohassett.	Jan. 29, 1855	Dis. to ch. in Quincy, Ill.
588	Martha (Hall) Clark (Rollin)	"	Profession of Faith.	Oct. 1, 1841	Dis. to ch. in Chester.
589	Tryphenia Walker	"	Letter from ch. Crown Point, N.Y.	Aug. 28, 1846	Dis. to Pres. ch. Collinsville, Ill.
				Oct. 15, 1837	Dis. to Preac.ch. Crown Point, N.Y.

No.	Name	Date	Mode	Date	Remarks
590	Susan Rice	Jan. 25, 1835	Letter from ch. Crown Point, N. Y.	April 30, 1858	Exc. See Church Records.
591	Nathaniel Holden (Nath.)	Feb. 22, 1835	Profession of Faith.	July 1, 1841	By death, aged years.
592	Hannah (Parker) Holden (Nath.)	"	"		Dis. to ch. in "
593	Calvin Durrent	March 1, 1835.	"	June 4, 1847	Exc. See Church Records.
594	Samuel Steele jr.	"	"	May 26, 1839	Dis. to ch. in Weathersfield E.
595	Sophia (Holden) Steele (Sam. jr.)	"	"	June 28, 1838	Dis. to ch. in Stockbridge.
596	Daniel Locke	"	"		Dis. to ch. in "
597	Elothia (Durrent) Locke (Daniel)	"	"	May 1, 1835	Dis. to ch. in "
598	George Pratt	"	"	April 8, 1842	Exc. See Church Records.
599	George Johnson	"	"		
600	Sarah Woodbury	"	"	April 13, 1838	By death, aged 25 years.
601	Joann Woodbury	"	"	Feb. 23, 1865	By death, aged 65 years.
602	Mary Gill	"	"	Oct. 11, 1835	Dis. to ch. in Felicity, O.
603	Albert Stevens	"	"		"
604	Alfred Stevens	"	"		"
605	George Stevens	May 3, 1835	"		"
606	Levi P. Morton	"	"	Feb. 1, 1836	Dis. to ch. in Winchendon, Ms.
607	Samuel Dyke	"	"	April 6, 1830	Dis. to ch. in Weathersfield E.
608	Z. W. Furber (Dr.)	"	"	July 24, 1835	Dis. to ch. in Charlestown, N. H.
609	Caroline (Edgerton) Furber (Dr. Z. W.)	"	"	"	"
610	Prudence (Stevens) Bingham (Hiram)	"	"		"
611	Talitha Stevens	"	"		"
612	Harriet (Oakes) Hubbard (John)	"	"		"
613	Nancy Hubbard	"	"		"
614	Fanny (Bowen) Heaton (Joseph)	"	"		"
615	Keziah Heaton	"	"		"
616	Nancy Heaton	"	"		"
617	Ann Eliza Hubbard	"	"	Jan. 4, 1839	Dis. to ch. in Guildhall.
618	Emily (Whitney) Closson (Judge Henry)	June 16, 1835	Letter from ch. in Marlboro.	Nov. 20, 1842	Dis. to ch. in Weathersfield E.
619	Lucius Matthews Pierce	July 3, 1835	Profession of Faith.	Nov. 10, 1850	By death, aged 74 years.
620	Henry Prentiss	"	"	April 4, 1861	By death, aged 84 years.
621	Mary (Pratt) Prentiss (Henry)	"	"	June 28, 1862	By death, aged 78 years.
622	Atalanta (Shafter) Hall (Caleb)	"	"	March 20, 1855	By death, aged years.
623	Jemima Walker	"	"	Feb. 1, 1855	Dis. to Bapt. ch. N. Springfield.
624	Nancy (Hayden) Thurston (Elmer)	"	"	March 28, 1863	By death, aged 45 years.
625	Martha (Hayden) Leland (Octavus)	"	"	July 24, 1835	Dis. to ch. in Charlestown, N. H.
626	Abel Miles	"	"		"
627	Elizabeth (Shipley) Miles (Abel)	"	"		"
628	Cynthia ( ) Munsell ( )	"	"		"
629	Mary Munsell	"	"		"
630	John Grear	"	"		"
631	Halford Earls'	"	"		"
632	Deborah (Marble) Eaton (Asa)	Sept. 6, 1835	Letter from ch. in Chester. Profession of Faith.	Feb. 22, 1860	By death, aged 83 years.

No.	Name.	Date of Recept'n.	Manner of Reception	Date of Removal.	Manner of Removal.
633	Susanna ( ) Wicker ( )	Nov. 29, 1835	Profession of Faith.	April 1, 1836	By death, aged years.
634	Catharine(White)(Stoddard)(Elijah) Reynolds (Elij.)	"	"		By death, aged 62 years.
635	Laura Hubbard	"	"	Jan. 4, 1839	Dis. to ch. in Guildhall.
636	Emily (Eaton) Putnam (Timothy)				
637	John Cotton Smith	Jan. 3, 1836	Letter from ch.in Claremont,N.H.		Dis. to ch. in Marion, O.
638	Abby ( ) Smith (John C.)	"	"	July 5, 1850	By death, aged 43 years.
639	Eliza (Fisher) Barnard (Henry)	Sept. 3, 1836.	Profession of Faith.	Feb. 20, 1857	Exc. See Church Records.
640	Elisha Sturtevant	Nov. 6, 1836	Letter from ch. in Dunstable, Ms.	Sept. 20, 1839	Dis. to ch. in Ware, Ms.
641	Mary ( ) Sturtevant (Elisha)	"	"	Jan. 11, 1843	Dis. to ch. in W. Brookfield,Ms.
642	Harriet (Butler) Holmes (Rev. H. B.)	"	Letter from ch.in Sunderland,Ms.	Feb. 11, 1844	Dis. to ch. in Shiloh, Ill.
643	Elizabeth (Pomeroy) Smith (Daniel)	"	Profession of Faith.	Aug. 31, 1862	By death, aged 32 years.
644	Lucretia Williams	Dec. 30, 1836	Letter from ch. in Saratoga, N. Y.	Aug. 27, 1859	
645	Leura (Haskins) Lewis (Dea. I. M.)	"	Letter from ch. in Jericho.		
646	Lucy (Carroll) Clement (Solomon)	March 3, 1837	Letter from ch. in Croydon.N. H	June 18, 1848	Dis. to ch. in Croydon. N. H.
647	Sarah M.(Forbush) Durren (Edmund)	March 17, 1837	Letter from ch. in Weathersfield.	Feb. 11, 1850	Dis. to ch. in Charlestown, Ms.
648	John S. Thompson	April 30, 1837	Profession of Faith.	1865	By death, aged 93 years.
649	De Witt Clinton Whitcomb	"	"	March 6, 1846	Exc. See Church Records.
650	Betsey (Glazier) Spencer (Jonas B.)	"	"	March 2, 1838	Exc. See Church Records.
651	Sarah Ann Rumrill	"	"	March 2, 1838	Exc. See Church Records.
652	Joseph Selden Jr.	June 29 1837	Letter f. ch. in Brownstown, Mich.	Nov. 29, 1860	By death, aged years.
653	Olive (Whitcomb) Selden (Joseph)	"	"	March 20, 1858	Dis.to Pres.c. Brownstown,Mich
654	Joseph Warren	Nov. 5, 1637	Letter from ch. in Peru.	April 15, 1853	Dis. to ch.in Lodi, Mich.
655	Jesse Warren	"	"	April 5, 1845	Dis. to ch.in Genoa Falls, N. Y.
656	Betsey (Jackson) Warren (Jesse)	"	"		
657	Leverett M. Snell	Jan. 12, 1838	Profession of Faith.	Oct. 4, 1867	Dis. to ch. in Springfield, Ill.
658	George D. Burgess (435)	"	Letter from Pres. ch. W. Union, O.	Oct. 23, 1838	Dis. to ch.in Troy, O.
659	Chauncey H. Smith	March 2, 1838	Letter f.F.W.B.ch.Haverhill,N.H.		Dis. to ch. in
660	Isaac Wisewall	"	Profession of Faith.		
661	Rosetta (Manly) Wisewall (Isaac)	"	Letter from ch. in Dorset.		
662	Elizabeth (Woodbury) Hubbard (Dr. C.)	"	Letter from ch.in Nelson, N. H.	Nov. 22, 1857	By death, aged 45 years.
663	Harriet (Johnson) Fisher (Isaac)	Aug. 8, 1838	Profession of Faith.		
664	Mary S. (James) (Joy) (Elisha) Whitcomb (Sam.)	Nov. 2, 1838	Letter from ch. in Cohasset, Ms.	Nov. 6, 1859	Dis. to ch. in Poughkeepsie,N. Y.
665	John Hall	"	Profession of Faith.		
666	George P. Haywood (Dea.)	"	"		
667	Caleb C. Burgess	Jan. 6, 1839	Letter from ch. in Newbury.	Aug. 15, 1847	Dis. to 3d ch. in Nashua, N. H.
668	Hiram Tyrell	"	"	Feb. 28, 1868	By death, aged 60 years.
669	Mary A. (Robinson) Tyrell (Hiram)	"	"		
670	George M. Wilder	"	Profession of Faith.	Jan. 31, 1840	Dis. to ch. in Dorchester, Ms.

	Date of Admission	Profession of Faith.	Date	Remarks
671 Marcia (Smith) Sawyer (Dr. Langdon)	Jan. 6, 1839		March 23, 1862	By death, aged 42 years.
672 Annziah Richmond	March 3, 1830	"	June 20, 1842	Dis. to ch. in Amesbury, Ms.
673 Harriet (Blackburn) Richmond (Am.)	"			
674 David Brown	"			Dis. to Prot. Ep. ch. Hartford, Ct.
675 Eliza Maria Adams	"			Exc. See Church Records.
676 William Davis	"		May 6, 1849	Dis. to ch. in Jordan, N. Y.
677 Amelia Maria (Russell) Davis (Wm.) (796)	"		Sept. 4, 1840	Dis. to ch. in Washington, D. C.
678 Sarah (Williams) Smiley (David)	"		April 4, 1866	
679 Nancy (Connut) Fairbanks ( )	"		Aug. 18, 1850	Dis. to Pres. ch. In Pottsville, Pa.
680 Harriet N. (Whitcomb) Shaeffer (Peter)	"		June 23, 1848	By death, aged 23 years.
681 Elizabeth Ann Burgess	April 21, 1839		July 1, 1840	Dis. to ch. in West Rutland.
682 Daniel Bailey Pratt	"		Oct. 5, 1841	By death, aged 69 years.
683 Alexander Grout (Dea.)	"		March 13, 1853	By death, aged 78 years.
684 Esther (Fisher) Grout (Dea. Alex.)	May 3, 1839	Letter from ch. in Acworth, N. H.	Sept. 1, 1856	Dis. to ch. in Lawrence, Kansas.
685 Sophia (Grout) Grimes (James A.)	"		July 20, 1850	By death, aged 35 years.
686 Lucy B. (Griswold) Goodenow (El. W.)	"		May 3, 1844	Dis. to ch. in Chester.
687 Abraham Whitcomb	"	Letter from ch. in Weathersfield.		
688 James Brush Whipple	"	Profession of Faith.		
689 Abigail (Davis) (Barnard) (Solon) Haskell (Perry)	"			
690 Mary Elizabeth McClenthan	May 31, 1839	Letter from ch. In Redford, Mich.	April 18, 1842	Dis. to ch in Quincy, Ms.
691 Allen Bates (255)	"	"	Jan. 1, 1843	Dis. to ch. in Redford, Mich.
692 Anna (Bates) Bates (Allen) (256)	July 5, 1839	Profession of Faith.	April 30, 1858	Exc. See Church Records.
693 Amy (Bixby) Damon (Hiram)	Oct. 27, 1839	Letter from ch. in Chester, N. H.	March 2, 1860	Dis. to ch in Westminster W.
694 James Dinsmore				
695 Zilpha (Taylor) Dinsmore (James)	Nov. 17, 1839	Letter from ch. ip Limerick, Me.	Oct. 29, 1843	By death, aged 71 years.
696 Beulah (Holton) White (John)	Feb. 28, 1840	Letter f. ch. Michigan City, Mich.	March 17, 1851	Dis. to ch. in Oswegatchie, N. Y.
697 Polly (Joiner) (McKinstry) (Alvin) Chaplin (David)	March 1, 1840	Profession of Faith.	March 1, 1844	
698 Rebecca (Gleason) Dinsmore (Henry)	May 4, 1840			
699 Calvin Hubbard (Dr.)	"		July 1, 1854	Dis. to ch. In Knoxville, Tenn.
700 Thomas Harkness Smiley	"			Dis. to ch. in Sullivan, N. H.
701 George Solon Kemp	"		Sept. 11, 1849	By death, aged 32 years.
702 Solon Barnard	"		Oct. 2, 1846	Exc. See Church Records.
703 Alfred Damon	"		Dec. 7, 1849	Exc. See Church Records.
704 Frederic G. Barnard	"		June 17, 1840	Dis. to ch. in North Troy.
705 Mary (Wright) Haywood ( )	"			
706 Gratia Burke	"			
707 Hannah (Cutler) Wood (Harvey)	Oct. 30, 1840	Letter from ch. in Redford, N. H.	Dec. 1, 1844	By death, aged 24 years.
708 Charles Aiken	"	Letter from ch. in Campton, N. H.	June 11, 1843	Dis. to ch. in Middlebury.
709 Adeline (Willey) Aiken (Charles)	"	Letter from ch. in Keene, N. H.		
710 Gardner Wilson	Jan. 1, 1841		Jan. 1, 1847	Dis. to ch. in Keene, N. H.
711 Martha A. F. ( ) Wilson Gardner	"			
712 Emeline (Jewett) Noble (Rev. Calvin D.)	"	Letter from ch. in Rochester.	Sept. 20, 1846	By death, aged 36 years.
713 Hannah (Davis) Whitney (Caleb)	"	Letter from ch. in Lowell, Ms.	April 30, 1858	Exc. See Church Records.

No.	Name.	Date of Recept'n.	Manner of Reception.	Date of Removal.	Manner of Removal.
714	Mary A. (Williams) Davis (Isaac G.)	Jan. 1, 1841	Letter from ch. in Perkinsville.	April 16, 1863	By death, aged 44 years.
715	Benjamin Parnell	"	"	Dec. 22, 1844	Dis. to ch. in Putney.
716	Mary (Sartwell) (Ward) (John) Parnell (Benj.)	"	"		"
717	Martha Ann (Parnell) Holden ( )	"	"	Aug. 4, 1833	"
718	Elijah Burke	"	Profession of Faith	March 22, 1843	By death, aged 69 years.
719	Mary Mitchell	"	"	March 1, 1842	By death, aged 23 years.
720	Jemison Barnard	"	"	Dec. 16, 1864	By death, aged 90 years.
721	Richard Knapp	"	"	Aug. 4, 1843	Exc. See Church Records.
722	Rhoda Ann (Dodge) Knapp (Richard)	"	"	Jan. 1, 1859	Dis. to ch. in Charlestown, N. H.
723	Samuel H. Burgess	"	"	Feb. 11, 1849	Dis. to Pearl St. ch. Nashua, N. H.
724	Daniel Smith	"	"	Aug. 31, 1862	Dis. to ch. in Shiloh, Ill.
725	Charles H. Rice	"	"	May 28, 1869	Dis. to M. E. ch. in Chelsea, Ms.
726	William E. Burgess	"	"	April 23, 1848	Dis. to 1st ch. in Lowell, Ms.
727	Russell Williams Burke	"	"	Jan. 4, 1863	Dis. to Prot. E. ch. Pittsburg, Pa.
728	Mark Richards Porter	"	"	Aug. 11, 1848	By death, aged 26 years.
729	Chester W. Johnson	"	"	July 14, 1844	Dis. to ch. in Boscawen, N. H.
730	Louisa M. (Senter) Johnson (Chester W.)	"	"		
731	Hosea W. Dodge	"	"	April 30, 1858	Exc. See Church Records.
732	Lyman Dodge	"	"	March 2, 1849	Dis. to ch. in Saxton's River.
733	Stoddard Tower	"	"	March 21, 1868	By death, aged 76 years
734	George Woodbury	"	"		
735	Mary Ann (Bates) Woodbury (George)	"	"		
736	Charles Farnsworth	"	"	May 14, 1846	Exc. See Church Records.
737	Louisa (Dutton) Farnsworth (Chas.)	"	"	April 30, 1858	"
738	Henry David Haywood	"	"	Nov. 26, 1847	Exc. See Church Records.
739	Lucy M. Clement	"	"	March 2, 1849	Dis. to ch. in Croydon, N. H.
740	Lucy T. Glynn	"	"	Aug. 1857	Dis. to ch. in
741	Martha (Foggett) Howe (Charles)	"	"	Nov. 15, 1844	Exc. See Church Records.
742	Lucy (Perkins) Litchfield (Otis B.)	"	"	Nov. 16, 1863	By death, aged 64 years.
743	Eliza Jane (Bodertha) Alvord (Solomon)	"	"	Jan. 1, 1848	Dis. to ch. in E. Hampton, Ms.
744	Thankful (Pomeroy) King (Arthur S.)	"	"	Jan. 30, 1852	Dis. to Pres. ch. in Chili, Ill.
745	Betsey S. (Tower) Manson (Samuel T.)	"	"		
746	Marcia (Spencer) Grinnell (Abel)	"	"	April 14, 1867	Dis. to ch. in Rehoboth, Md.
747	Esther (Spencer) Grout (Daniel)	"	"		
748	Sophia W. Murfee	"	"	April 30, 1858	Exc. See Church Records.
749	Lucretia (Bodertha) Porter (George W.)	"	"		
750	Rosanna (Ellis) Pratt (Daniel B.)	"	"	Feb. 20, 1853	Dis. to ch. in Hastings, Mich.
751	Eliza Ann (Ellis) Pratt (Daniel B.)	"	"	June 5, 1855	"

No.	Name	Admitted	Profession of Faith	Removed	Remarks
752	Eliza (Brown) Olney (Welcome)	Jan. 1, 1841	Profession of Faith	March 1, 1844	Exc. See Church Records.
753	Mary A. Blanchard (Sylvanus)	"	"	Feb. 8, 1841	Dis. to Pres. ch. in Troy, N. Y.
754	Nancy F. Grout	"	"	Sept. 7, 1841	By death, aged 60 years.
755	Mary (Rogers) Cabot (Hubbard)	"	"	Jan. 1, 1846	Dis. to ch. in Detroit, Mich.
756	Rebecca Dutton	"	"	Nov. 15, 1844	Exc. See Church Records.
757	Catharine G. (Bates) Smith (Charles)	"	"	July 2, 1847	Exc. See Church Records.
758	Orinda E. (Woods) France (Hermon E.)	"	"	July 18, 1855	By death, aged 27 years.
759	Lucina (Tuft) Moore (George)	"	"		
760	Gratia Ann (Holman) Jones (George W.)	"	"		
761	Augusta A. (Damon) Hall (Edward)	Jan. 15, 1841	"	Sept. 3, 1853	By death, aged 81 years.
762	Jonathan Williams	"	"	Jan. 23, 1841	By death, aged 67 years.
763	Elizabeth (Kidder) Williams (Jona)	March 7, 1841	"	Feb. 28, 1841	Dis. to ch. in
764	Mary Lovina Lull	"	"		
765	Daniel Cushing	"	Letter from ch. in Quechee.	Oct. 20, 1864	By death, aged 68 years.
766	Nancy (Anthony) Cushing (Daniel)	"	"	Oct. 26, 1854	By death, aged 43 years.
767	Nancy (Sherwin) Bates (Phinehas)	"	Letter from ch. in Perkinsville.	April 24, 1860	Dis. to Pres. ch. in Rehoboth, Md.
768	Abel H. Grinnell	"	Profession of Faith.	June 18, 1848	Dis. to ch. in Croydon, N. H.
769	Solomon Clement	"	"		
770	Henry Closson (Judge)	"	"		
771	Martha Fronty	"	"		
772	Gratia Ann (Tower) Bennett (Charles)	"	"	Nov. 24, 1849	Exc. See Church Records.
773	Clementine (Merritt) (Haseltine) (S.) Edson (Ezra)	"	"	May 13, 1863	By death, aged 67 years.
774	Lucretia (Farwell) Derby (Samuel)	"	"	Sept. 15, 1864	By death, aged 31 years.
775	Mary Ann Derby	"	"	Nov. 26, 1862	By death, aged 31 years.
776	Nancy (Cushing) Safford (Henry)	"	"	Nov. 15, 1844	Exc. See Church Records.
777	John Miller	"	"	March 25, 1855	Dis. to ch. in Evansville, Wis.
778	Harriet (Rogers) Roynton (Wayland)	"	"	Aug. 18, 1850	Dis. to ch. in Weston.
779	Sarah Lincoln (Ellis) Clark (Horace L.)	"	"		
780	Gratia Ann Chipman	"	"		
781	Lucia Maria (Snell) Whitcomb (Henry)	May 2, 1841	"	Jan. 30, 1850	Dis. to ch. in Derby.
782	Harriet Ann (Davis) Davis (Luke)	"	"	Nov. 15, 1844	Exc. See Church Records.
783	Cynthia Ann (Fairbanks) Kendall ( )	July 11, 1841	Letter from ch. in Walpole, N. H.		
784	Lincoln Whitcomb	"	Profession of Faith.		
785	Jeremiah Ellis	"	"	Dec. 15, 1856	By death, aged 56 years.
786	Hannah (Whitcomb) Ellis (Jeremiah)	Sept. 5, 1841	Letter from ch. in Windham.		
787	George W. Fletcher	"	Profession of Faith.	April 30, 1858	Exc. See Church Records.
788	Zeno E. Spring	"	Letter from ch. in Quechee.	April 17, 1853	Dis. to ch. in Framingham, Ill.
789	Arvilla (Gould) Spring (Zeno E.)	"	Letter f. ch. in Newburyport, Ms.		
790	David M. Washburn	Jan. 1, 1842	Profession of Faith.	April 30, 1858	Exc. See Church Records.
791	Zeruiah (Chamberlain Cushing (Daniel)	"	"	March 17, 1852	By death, aged 85 years.
792	Lydia Ann (Emerson) Porter (Charles E.)	"	"	Dec. 8, 1863	Dis. to ch. in Putnam, O.
793	Sophronia P. (Henry) Downs (Chas.)	"	Profession of Faith.	Aug. 30, 1846	Dis. to ch. in Manchester, N. H.
794	Betsey Davis	Feb. 14, 1842	Letter from ch. in Weathersfield.		

No.	Name.	Date of Recept'n.	Manner of Reception.	Date of Removal.	Manner of Removal.
795	Elvira Davis	Feb. 14, 1842	Profession of Faith.	Sept. 15, 1844	By death, aged 35 years.
796	Amelia Maria [Bissell] Davis [Wm.] [	Nov. 6, 1842	Letter from ch. in Jordan, N. Y.	Jan. 24, 1869	Dis. to ch. in Elkhart, Ind.
797	Joseph Whiting	"	Profession of Faith.	July 14, 1868	By death, aged 70 years.
798	John P. Eaton	"	"		
799	Hermon E. France	"	"	Nov. 15, 1844	Exc. See Church Records.
800	Charles C. Thornton	"	"	May 6, 1849	Exc. See Church Records.
801	Timothy Putnam	"	"		
802	Asa Eaton	"	"	Aug. 17, 1866	By death, aged 80 years.
803	Solomon H. Clement	"	"	March 2, 1849	Dis. to ch. in Croydon, N. H.
804	Edward Hall	"	"		
805	Alonzo Chipman	"	"	April 30, 1858	Exc. See Church Records.
806	David R. Smiley	"	"	April 4, 1866	Dis. to ch. in Washington, D. C.
807	Samuel D. Hill	"	"		Dis. to ch. in Proctorsville,
808	James C. Bradburn	"	"	April 30, 1858	Exc. See Church Records.
809	James L. Sargent	"	"		Exc. See Church. Records.
810	George Hunter	"	"		
811	Elhanan W. Goodenow	"	"	Oct. 30, 1868	Exc. See Church Records.
812	Albert Davis	"	"		
813	Ephraim Wright	"	"	Nov. 29, 1867	Dis.to M.E. ch. Claremont, N. H.
814	Edward Cushing	"	"		Dis. to ch. in Houston, Texas.
815	James L. Walker	"	"	March 20, 1847	Exc. See Church Records.
816	Dara Graham	"	"		
817	Charles L. Cobb	"	"	June 1, 1843	Dis.to Cen. ch. Kalamazoo, Mich.
818	Samuel Haywood	"	"	Feb. 13, 1846	Exc. See Church Records.
819	James Haywood	"	"	March 20, 1846	Exc. See Church Records.
820	Thomas L. Jenkins	"	"		
821	Charles E. Porter	"	"		
822	James Spencer	"	"	April 10, 1859	By death, aged 52 years.
823	Henry W. Closson [Col.]	"	"	April 30, 1858	Exc. See Church Records
824	Henry Safford	"	"		
825	Joseph Whitcomb Ellis	"	"	Jan. 13, 1851	Exc. See Church Records.
826	Arthur C. Whitcomb	"	"	Sept. 10, 1851	By death, aged 20 years.
827	Daniel A. Grout	"	"	June 5, 1846	Exc. See Church Records.
828	Samuel Derby	"	"		
829	Lois [Hardy] Rice [Benjamin]	"	"		
830	Matilda A. [Rice] (Grimes [Jones]	"	"		
831	Emily J. [Graham] Eaton [John P.]	"	"		
832	Adeline [Whiting] Cutler [Enos]	"	"	March 11, 1863	By death, aged 78 years.

No. Name		Profession of Faith.		Remarks
833	Mary W. Whiting	Nov. 6, 1842	April 5, 1849	By death, aged 22 years.
834	Mary A. Tyrell	"	Nov. 15, 1841	Exc. See Church Records.
835	Lucia W. [Tyrell] Lewis [Benjamin A.]	"		Exc. See Church Records.
836	Bethiah [Spencer] Knight [Joseph]	"		
837	Sarah E. [Brown][Breck][Dr.Jos.B.]Wardner[Clark]	"	Jan. 8, 1846	Exc. See Church Records.
838	Sarah J. Whitcomb	"	June 20, 1869	Dis.to Winthrop ch.Charleston, Ms.
839	Sarah Maria [Clark] Bates [Moses J.]	"	July 26, 1863	By death, aged 31 years. [Ms.
840	Eliza Davis	"	1844	By death, aged 20 years.
841	Laura Edson	"		
842	Lucy Ann [Clark] Whiting [Samuel]	"		
843	Mary A. [Whitcomb] Whipple [James B.]	"		
844	Louisa [Wright] Minot [	"		
845	Phebe F. Belknap	"		By death, aged years.
846	Tryphene Dinsmore	"		
847	Nancy [Rumrill] Holden [William M.]	"	March 8, 1840	Dis. to ch. In Proctorsville.
848	Eliza A. Hill [Samuel]	"		Dis. to M. E. ch. in Springfield.
849	Sarah Elizabeth Fairbanks	"	March 6, 1849	Exc. See Church Records.
850	Tila O. [Eaton] Tower [John]	"	Oct. 1, 1855	Dis. to ch. In Wrentham, Ms.
851	Martha W. [Thornton] Ward [Cyrus]	"		
852	Eunice [Cook] Williams [Luke]	"		
853	Maria Davis	"		
854	Lydia [Ronld] Spring [Luther]	"	April 8, 1852	By death, aged 32 years.
855	Sarah J. Wheelock	"	Sept. 2, 1849	Dis. to ch. in Grafton, Me.
856	Lucia J. Cobb	"	Jun. 22, 1845	Dis. to Cen. ch.Kalamazoo,Mich.
857	Mary Jane Whitney	"	Sept. 14, 1847	By death, aged 22 years.
858	Emily Safford [Glossen] Fellows [Dr. A. M.]	"		
859	Caroline Farrar	"	March 25, 1846	By death, aged 25 years.
860	Jane [Pratt] Marble [Thomas]	"	May 29, 1859	By death, aged 63 years.
861	Julia F. [Hemminway] Taylor [Luke]	"		
862	Susan [McRae] Spencer [James]	"	April 30, 1858	Exc. See Church Records.
863	Phebe [Richardson][Haywood][Cyrus] Swift [John]	"		
864	Harriet M. Derby	"	March 29, 1849	By death, aged 20 years.
865	Tryphena M. Thornton	"	Feb. 27, 1861	By death, aged 33 years.
866	Martha B. [Williams] Crain [Frederic]	"		
867	William M. Messinger	Jan. 1, 1843	Letter from Ref. M.ch. Springfield. Sept. 2, 1849	By death, aged 39 years.
868	Arabella S. [Field] Messinger [Wm. M.]	"	Profession of Faith. Aug. 17, 1865	By death, aged 49 years.
869	Daniel Taft	"	" May 14, 1856	Exc. See Church Records.
870	Sophronia Taft	"	" "	Exc. See Church Records.
871	Susan [Merritt] Field [Salathiel]	"	Dec. 24, 1862	By death, aged 69 years.
872	Clarissa [Weston] Whiting [Joseph]	"	Oct. 2, 1856	By death, aged 58 years.
873	Orinda [Courser] Shaw [Daniel]	"	May 6, 1869	By death, aged 59 years.
874	Mary Ann [Merritt] Wisewall [Isaac]	"		
875	Lewis W. Harlow	"	Nov. 24, 1840	Exc. See Church Records.

38

No.	Name.	Date of Recept'n.	Manner of Reception.	Date of Removal.	Manner of Removal.
876	Laura [Bellows] Harlow [Lewis W.]	Jan. 1, 1843	Profession of Faith.	April 30, 1858	Exc. See Church Records.
877	Susan [Fisher] Chase [Jona.]	"	"	Sept. 1864	By death, aged 67 years.
878	Betsey Mitchell	"	"	Sept. 5, 1864	By death, aged 67 years.
879	Calvin S. White	"	"	Nov. 26, 1847	Exc. See Church Records.
880	Marcia Field				
881	Louisa Thornton Ward				
882	Hannah L. [Tracy] Coffin [	July 2, 1843	"	Nov. 26, 1847	Exc. See Church Records.
883	Mary K. [Whipple] [Harlow] [W. B.] Davis [I. G.]	Aug. 25, 1843	Letter from ch. in	Oct. 31, 1852	Dis. to M. E. ch. Claremont, N.H.
884	Aurelia S. Liscomb	"	"	"	"
885	Father Ann Liscomb				
886	Relief B.[Stickney] Wood [Jona.B.]	Sept. 23, 1843	Profession of Faith.	Jan. 20, 1844	By death, aged 68 years.
887	William K. Grout	Nov. 5, 1843	"	May 9, 1860	By death, aged 54 years.
888	Nancy J. [Haywood] Grout [Wm. K.]	"		May 28, 1869	Dis. to ch. In Quechee.
889	Elizabeth [Phelps] Atherton [Adonijah]	March 1, 1844	Letter from ch. in Quechee.	May 1, 1845	Dis. to ch. in Flint, Mich.
890	Maria [Phelps] Guild [Dr. James]			"	"
891	Lathrop Taylor [Rev.]	Nov. 2, 1845	Letter from ch. in Taunton, Ms.	1845	Dis. to ch. in Francistown, N.H.
892	Hannah T. [Hall] Taylor [Rev. L.]	"	"	1845	"
893	Ebenezer Adams Knight [Dr.]	May 10, 1849	Letter from ch. in Hancock, N.H.		
894	Mary [Wheeler] Knight [Dr. E. A.]	Sept. 6, 1848	Letter from ch. in Keene, N. H.	March 28, 1869	Dis. to 1st ch. in Keene, N. H.
895	Salmon Whitcomb				
896	Fanny [Selden] Whitcomb [Salmon]				
897	Mary B. Earle	Nov. 1, 1846	Letter from ch. in Chester.	May 6, 1849	By death, aged 29 years.
898	Benjamin Parnell	"	Letter from ch. in Putney.	March 10, 1848	By death, aged 76 years.
899	Mary [Sartwell] [Ward] [John] Parnell [Benj.]			Jan. 22, 1854	By death, aged 74 years.
900	Maria P. [Munn] Rice [Daniel]	Jan. 1, 1846	Letter from ch. in Dummerston.		
901	Calvin Munn	"			
902	Mehitable [Fletcher] Porter [Sam.] Munn [Calvin]	"	Letter from Pr. ch. Saratoga, N.Y.	May 3, 1850	By death, aged 80 years.
903	Clarissa [Jewett] Wilcox [Augustus]	"	Letter from ch. in Chester.	Aug. 19, 1853	By death, aged 84 years.
904	Arabel [Earls] Fiske [Jerome]				
905	Lucy M. [Earls] Smith [Alvah]				
906	James A. Grimes	April 30, 1847	Letter from M. E. ch. Springfield.	Sept. 1, 1855	Dis. to ch. in Lawrence, Kas.
907	Sarah [Grimes] Gilson [Joel]	"	Profession of Faith.	June 27, 1858	By death, aged 86 years.
908	Amelia [Smith] Spencer [Peter]	July 4, 1847	Letter from ch.in Claremont, N.H.	Jan. 1, 1851	Dis. to ch. in Claremont N.H.
909	Amasa Woolson [Dea.]	Sept. 5, 1847	Letter from ch. in Chester.		
910	Mary [Davidson] Woolson [Amasa]	"	Letter from ch.in Stafford, Canada.	April 16, 1862	By death, aged 47 years.
911	Mary M. [Bowker] Baker [Dr. Justus]	"	Letter from ch. in Hancock, N.H.	April 11,1854	Dis. to Bap.ch. in Bellows Falls.
912	Maria [Foster] Sherwin [Jona.]	May 7, 1848	Letter from ch. in Hancock, N.H.	Dec. 23, 1853	Dis. to ch. in Grafton.
913	Mary L. [Warner] Wright [John T.]	Jan. 7, 1849	Letter from ch. in Saxton's River,	April 30, 1858	Dis. with general Letter.

No. and Name	Date received	Manner of admission	Date of dismission or death	Remarks
914 Catherine [Shattuck] [Kimball] [Geo.] Brown [Luke]	May 6, 1849	Letter from ch. in Temple, N. H.	June 8, 1865	By death, aged 93 years.
915 Selah R. Arms [Rev.]	"	Letter from ch. in Windham.	Nov. 9, 1860	By death, aged 77 years.
916 Eliza [Ames] Arms [Rev. S. R.]	"	"	Dec. 22, 1861	By death, aged 62 years.
917 Maria Pratt Arms	"	"	July 1, 1866	Dis. to ch. in Townshend.
918 James Lovell	Sept. 2, "	Letter from ch. in Chester.		
919 Lucretia O. [Whitney] Lovell [James]	"	"	July 29, 1853	By death, aged 38 years.
920 Thomas Marble Merritt [1214]	"	"	May 12, 1867	Dis. to M. E. ch. in Springfield.
921 Hannah [Aldrich] Aldrich [Edward]	"	"	Feb. 17, 1850	Dis. to ch. in Westmoreland, N.H.
922 Henrietta E. Williams	"	"	April 30, 1858	Dis. to ch. in Alton, Ill.
923 Elizabeth [Davis] Forbush [Chas. A.]	Sept. 9, 1849	"		
924 Sophia [Graves] Holman [Smith]	"	"	Jan. 20, 1851	By death, aged 67 years.
925 Hannah Gould	Nov. 4, 1849	Profession of Faith.		
926 Frances O. [Whitcomb] Hall [Benj.]	"	Profession of Faith.	March 20, 1858	Dis. to ch. In Flat Rock, Mich.
927 Edward P. Anthony	Jan. 6, 1850	Letter from ch. in Hatfield, Ms.	July 1, 1855	Dis. to ch. in Hatfield, Ms.
928 Nelson W. Goddard	"	Letter from ch. in Chester.	Aug. 1, 1863	Dis. to ch. in Springfield, Ms.
929 Sarah D. [Gibson] Goddard [Nelson W.]	"	Profession of Faith.		"
930 Salina Maria Shaw	"	"		
931 Charles Sabin	March 3, 1850	Letter from ch. Fitzwilliam, N. H.	Dec. 5, 1856	Dis. to ch. In Rockford, Ill.
932 Abby [Cutter] Sabin [Charles]	"	"		"
933 Ashhel Steele [Dea.]	"	Letter from ch. Weathersfield E.		
934 Lucy M. [Barnard] Steele [Dea. A.]	"	"	Jan. 15, 1852	By death, aged 39 years.
935 Horatio G. Hawkins [Dea.]	July 7, 1850	Letter from ch. in Manchester.	Aug. 12, 1861	By death, aged 73 years.
936 Francis Kitchell	"	Profession of Faith.	April 30, 1858	Exc. See Church Records.
937 Eliza J. [Belknap] Meacham [Edgar A.]	July 6, 1851	Letter from ch. in Weathersfield.	Jan. 30, 1857	Dis. to ch. in Prescott, Wis.
938 John Chase [Dea.]	July 4, 1852	"		
939 Lucy [Sherwin] Chase [Dea. John]	"	"		
940 Mary E. [Hodgkins] Giddings [Rev. S. P.]	Sept. 5, 1852	Letter from ch. in New Haven, Ct.	Dec. 1, 1858	Dis. to ch. in Rutland.
941 Sarah [Austin] [Lovejoy] [Henj.] Davis [Dea. Wm.]	May 1, 1853	Letter from ch. in Weston.	July 1, 1868	By death, aged 70 years.
942 Rachel [Tower] Bates [Davis]	Sept. 1, 1853	Letter from ch. in Chester.	Nov. 15, 1868	By death, aged 73 years.
943 Drrilla [Newton] Loveland [John C.]	"	Letter from ch. in Hoosic, N.Y.	June 1, 1854	By death, aged 37 years.
944 Electa [Jowett] Steele [Dea. A.]	June 1, 1854	Letter from ch. in Middlebury.		
945 Henry F. Curiel [Dr.]	May 5, 1854	Letter from ch.Charlestown,N.H.	April 2, 1858	Dis. to ch. in Trenton, N. J.
946 Laura [Sawyer] [Hurd] [Calvin] Tower [Stoddard]	"	Letter from ch. in Newport, N.H.		
947 Sarah [Sawyer] Carter [ ]	May 7, 1854	Letter from ch. in		By death, aged years.
948 Almeria [Hyde] Lovell [James]	July 1, 1854	Letter from ch.Francistown, N.H.		
949 Frances [Noble] Swift [Foster]	May 6, 1855	Profession of Faith.	1861	Dis. to ch. in Bellows Falls.
950 William Dickinson	"	"	Nov. 23, 1856	Dis. to N. Eng. ch. Chicago, Ill.
951 Lydia [Hall] Burbank [Daniel]	"	Letter from ch. in Stockbridge.		
952 C. Augustus Watkins	"	Letter from ch. in Peru.	Jan. 1, 1864	Dis. to ch. in Ludlow.
953 Lizzie B. [Newton][Woodward][Dr.][Loveland][J. C.]	Nov. 4, 1855	Profession of Faith.	Jan. 19, 1864	By death, aged 44 years.
954 Helen Ann Woolson	"	"	Jan. 27, 1862	By death, aged 23 years.
955 Elvira [Winchester] Felt [Wells]	"	"	May 28, "	Dis. to Prot. E. ch. St. Louis, Mo.
956 Fanny [Arms] Goddard [Daniel]	"	"		Dis. to ch. in Townshend.

No.	Name.	Date of Recept'n.	Manner of Reception.	Date of Removal.	Manner of Removal.
957	Emily M. Arms	Nov. 4, 1855	Profession of Faith.	Jan. 1, 1861	Dis. to Mt. Vernon ch. Boston Ms.
958	Eunice [Richards] [Blake] [James] Gilson [Kiah]	Dec. 14, 1855	Letter from ch. in Rockingham.	Feb. 7, 1859	Dis. to Eliot ch. Lawrence, Ms.
959	Mary S. Litchfield	Jan. 6, 1856	Profession of Faith.	Aug. 13, 1862	By death, aged 45 years
960	Margaret Heachey	"	"		
961	Isaac Ellis	March 2, 1856	"	March 31, 1867	Dis. to M. E. ch. in Springfield.
962	Mary A. Ellis	May 4, 1856	"		
963	Anna Brown [Dea.]	"	"	July 5, 1861	By death, aged 32 years.
964	Mary A. [Newton] Brown [Dea.]	"	"		
965	William Walker	"	"		
966	Joseph Lansing	"	"	Dec. 3, 1859	Dis. to 1st ch. in Burlington.
967	Jane Maria Holden	"	"	Sept. 1, 1867	Dis. to Eliot ch. in Roxbury Ms.
968	Emily V. [Holden] Bates [Calvin]	"	"		
969	Elizabeth Holden	"	"		
970	Harriet E. Holden	"	"	March 28, 1860	By death, aged 24 years.
971	Elizabeth F. Derby	"	"		
972	Julia F. Ellis	"	"	Sept. 29, 1865	By death, aged 24 years.
973	Harriet A. [Cram] Porter [George C.]	"	"		
974	Eleanor P. [Whitcomb] Shaeffer [William]	"	"	Sept. 29, 1864	Dis. to ch. in Windham.
975	Laura Jane [Holman] Moore [Samuel]	"	"	Dec. 1, 1856	By death, aged 21 years.
976	Mary Holman	"	"		
977	Lucia A. [Lovell] Davis [Ira]	July 6, 1856	"		
978	Elizabeth H Hubbard	"	"		
979	Harriet L. [Hubbard] White [Joseph]	"	"	April 12, 1867	Dis. to ch. in Guildhall.
980	Catharine R. [Hubbard] Haywood [Henry]	"	"	Jan. 25, 1861	Dis. to Pres. ch. Seymour, Ill.
981	Ellen B. [Tower] Caldwell [Charles]	"	"	Feb. 18, 1866	Dis. to ch. in Portland Oregon.
982	Mary N. Tower	"	"		
983	Orin Locke [Dea.]	Sept. 5, 1856	Letter from ch. in Chester.	April 29 1860	Dis. to N. ch. Springfield, Ms.
984	Nancy [Williams] Locke [Dea. Orin]	"	"	June 21, 1866	By death, aged 31 years.
985	Eliza Arms	"	Profession of Faith.	July 31, 1857	Dis. to ch. in Brattleboro.
986	Olivia [Burke] Closson [Col. H. W.]	Sept. 7, 1856	"		
987	Henry W. Alexander	"	"		
988	Almira [Bodertha] [Caldwell] [J.P.] Safford [Noah]	Oct. 3, 1854	Letter from ch. E. Hampton, Ms.		
989	Sarah [Temple] [Farrington] [Abr.] Taylor [Samuel]	Nov. 1, 1856	Letter from ch. In Chester.		
990	Harriet [Brewer] Wheeler [William]	Jan. 4, 1857	Letter from ch. Fitzwilliam, N.H.		
991	Maria R. [Ellis] Spalding [Eri J.]	"	Profession of Faith.	April 24, 1868	Dis. to ch. in Milford, Ms.
992	George Bates Woodbury	"	"		
993	William Milton Holden	"	"		
994	John Jenison Burnard	March 1, 1857	Letter from ch. in Windham.		

No. / Name	Date	Mode of Admission	Date	Removal / Death
995 Thirza [Woodburn] Barnard [John J.] (215)	May 6, 1857	Letter from ch. in Windham,	1860	Dis. to ch. in Claremont, N. H.
996 Edna [Steele] Tenney [Rev. S. G.]	"	Letter from ch. in Lyndon.		
997 Elizabeth Lois [Tenney] Vaughan [Edwin]	July 5, 1857	Profession of Faith.		
998 Samuel Steele Jr.	"	Letter from ch. Weathersfield E.	Jan. 1, 1864	Dis. to ch. in Ludlow.
999 Mary C. [Waite] [Mather] [Chas.] Steele [Sam. Jr.]				
1000 Elizabeth T. [Goodrich] Watkins [G. Augustus]	Sept. 6, 1857	Profession of Faith.		
1001 Charles Haywood [Dea.]	"	Letter from ch. in Weathersfield.		
1002 Parthena [Newton] Haywood [Dea. Chas.]	Jan. 3, 1858	Profession of Faith.		
1003 Horace Weston Thompson	"	"		
1004 Mary M. [Whitcomb] Fullam [James]	July 4, 1858	Letter from ch. in Cavendish.	Dec. 1, 1862	Dis. to ch. in Ludlow.
1005 Malina W. [Loveland] Closson [Gershom L.]	Nov. 14, 1858	Letter from ch. in Proctorsville.		
1006 Ebenezer T. Weeks		Letter from ch. in Chester.		
1007 Anna [Parker] Gilson [Abel]	Feb. 20, 1859	Letter from ch. in Ottawa, Ill.		
1008 Samantha W. [Gilson] Andrews [Rev. Claudius]	Feb. 1, 1859	Letter from 1st ch. in Lowell, Ms.	Jan. 22, 1864	By death, aged 73 years.
1009 Lucretia [Bates] Cutler [Calvin D.]	July 1, 1859			
1010 Henry J. Parker				
1011 William Davidson [Dea.]	Sept. 4, 1859	Profession of Faith.		
1012 Hannah [Steele][Powers][Geo.] Davidson [Dea. Wm.]	"	"		
1013 John C. Loveland				
1014 John Gilman Tenney				
1015 John A. Slack	June 29, 1860	Letter from M. E. ch. Springfield.Ms.	Nov. 10, 1867	Dis. to M. E. ch. in Springfield.
1016 Rhoda J. [Page] Tyrell [Harlan]	Aug. 31, 1860	Letter from ch. in McIndoe's Falls.	Nov. 1, 1861	Dis. to ch. in Windsor.
1017 James Colburn Bowen	Nov. 2, 1860	Letter from bap. ch. in Felchville.		
1018 Mary E. [Downs] Bowen [James C.]		Letter from M. E. ch. Lowell. Ms.		
1019 Thomas Jameson [Rev.]	Jan. 4, 1861	Letter from ch. in Gorham, Me.	Jan. 1, 1864	Dis. to ch. in Greenland, N. H.
1020 John W. Chickering [Rev.]		Letter f. High St. ch.Portland.Me.	Jan. 1, 1866	Dis. to 2d ch. in Exeter, N. H.
1021 Lucinda [Jameson] Chickering [Rev. J. W.]		Letter from ch. in Gorham, Mo.		
1022 Minerva E. Lewis	Jan. 6, 1861	Profession of Faith.		
1023 Elizabeth [Burt] Pettingill [Tracy P.]	"	"	Nov. 29, 1867	Dis. to ch. in Philadelphia, Pa.
1024 Leroy M. Pierce	May 5, 1861	"	Feb. 21, 1869	Dis.to Pres.ch. in Lewisburg,Pa.
1025 Elizabeth F. [Abbott] Newton [R. D.]	July 5, 1861	"		
1026 Moses Coffin	Feb. 2, 1862	"	Sept. 8, 1867	Dis. to ch. in Redwood City,Cal.
1027 Lydia A. [Pierce] Snowden [Rev. B. R.]	Sept. 7, 1862	Letter from ch. in Ashland, Ms.	Jan. 10, 1866	By death, aged 23 years.
1028 Abby L. Hall	"	Profession of Faith.		
1029 Frederic Y. A. Townsend	Jan. 2, 1862	Letter from ch. in Norwich.		
1030 Amelia [Royce] Townsend [Fred. Y. A.]	"	Profession of Faith.		
1031 Abigail [Dutton] McCormick [Alexander]	Sept. 4, 1863	Letter from 1st ch. Springfield.Ms.	Aug. 25, 1863	By death, aged 51 years.
1032 George Bowers [b. D. S.]		Letter fr. Olive St.ch. Nashua,N.H.		
1033 Frania E. [Brackett] Bowers [Dr. George]		Letter from 1st ch.in Holyoke, Ms.		
1034 Mary [Baker] Woolson [Dea. Amasa]	Oct. 31, 1863	Letter from bap. ch. Manchester.		
1035 Addie Burgess	Jan. 3, 1864	Profession of Faith.	Jan. 31, 1864	By death, aged 20 years.
1036 Rachel J. [Codin] Messinger [Zimri]	"	"		
1037 Sarah Josephine Mudgett				

No.	Name.	Date of Recept'n.	Manner of Reception.	Date of Removal.	Manner of Removal.
1038	Mary R. (Nourse) Washburn (Pliny)	Jan. 3, 1864	Profession of Faith.	July 3, 1868	Dis. to Prot. Epis ch. in U.S.A.
1039	Eliza A. (Rice) (Warren) (Hez.) Butterfield (Chas.)	"	"		
1040	Lizzie A. (Chase) Walker (William)	"	"		
1041	Mary C. Chase	"	"		
1042	Caroline A.(Jackman)(Hatch)(Wm.D.) Coffin (Moses)	"	"		
1043	Nelson W. Locke	"	"		
1044	Fannie(Woolson) Brown (Dea. Adna)	"	Letter from ch. in Montpelier.		
1045	Merrill L. Lawrence (1100)	April 17, 1864	Profession of Faith.	Feb. 23, 1867	Dis. to M. E. ch. Llma, N. Y.
1046	Hattie Jane (Wilson) Nourse (Lucian R.)	Nov. 6, 1864	Letter from ch. in Putney.	Oct. 4, 1867	Dis. to ch. in Melrose, Ms.
1047	Olive L. (Houghton) Locke (Nelson W.)	"	Letter from ch. in Weathersfield.		
1048	Sarah L. Upham	"	Profession of Faith.		
1049	Mary Jane (Steele) Dunklee (Ellis W.)	"	"		
1050	Mary Augusta (Fay) Hall (George R.)	May 7, 1865	"	Sept. 13, 1868	Dis. to ch. in Norwich.
1051	Ariel Edgerton Goddard	"	Letter from ch. Weathersfield E.	Sept. 8, 1867	Dis. to ch. in Windham. "
1052	Charles Town	"	"		
1053	Susan S. (Ellis) Town (Charles)	"	Letter from ch. Lempster, N. H.		
1054	Caroline Frances (Parker) Booth (Frederic)	"	Letter f.Appleton St.ch.Lowell,Ms		
1055	Louisa (Bowen) Field (Lincoln)	"	Letter from M. E. ch. Springfield.		
1056	Mary (Chipman) Stearns (Charles E.)	"	Letter from ch. in Peru, Ms.		
1057	Olive Augusta (Goodrich) Derby (Farrington)	July 9, 1865	Profession of Faith.		
1058	Sarah C. Grinnell	Sept. 3, 1865	Letter from ch. in Lempster,N. H	April 14, 1867	Dis.to Pres.ch.in Rehoboth, Md.
1059	James Booth	Jan. 7, 1866			
1060	Marion E. (Parker) Booth (James)	"	Letter from ch.in Claremont, N.H.		
1061	Elizabeth F.(Husse)Philbrick)(John) Colcord(Daniel)	"	Letter from ch. in Lebanon, N.H.		
1062	Benjamin Burge Choate	"	Letter from ch. in Hartford.		
1063	Mary M. (Allard) Choate (Benj. B.)	March 4, 1866	Profession of Faith.	July 22, 1867	By death, aged 19 years
1064	Joseph Woodbury	"	"		
1065	Hattie N. Locke	"	"		
1066	Anna E.(Hatch) Washburn (Alphonzo G.)	May 6, 1866	Letter from ch. Weathersfield E.		
1067	Abby (Fifield) Safford (Henry)	Nov. 11, 1866	Profession of Faith		
1068	Juliette H. Fiske	Jan. 13, 1867	"		
1069	George R. Hall	May 5, 1867	"		
1070	Merrill N. (Bates) Aldrich (Samuel)	"	"		
1071	Abigail S. (Bates) Litchfield (Ansolum)	"	"		
1072	Frances Ann Woodbury	"	"		
1073	Levi Henry Cobb (Rev.)	"	"		
1074	Harriet Jane (Herrick) Cobb (Rev. L. H.)	"	Letter from ch. in Meriden, N.H.		
1075	Sarah (Gregg) Sawyer (Dr. Langlon)	"	Letter from ch. in Newport, N.H.		

No.	Name	Date	Manner of admission	Date	Remarks
1076	Elizabeth B. McDonald	May 6, 1867	Profession of Faith.	Sept. 8, 1867	Dis to ch. in Malone, N. Y.
1077	Maria Pratt Arms	"	Letter from ch. in Townshend.		
1078	Sybil (Bar) Barrett (Charles)	"	Letter from ch. in Weathersfield.		
1079	Edward Ingham	"	Letter from ch. in Norwich.		
1080	Edward Arthur Booth	July 5, 1867	Letter from ch. in Lempster, N.H.	Dec. 24, 1867	Dis. to ch. in Wabasha, Minn.
1081	Samuel Gilman Tenney (Rev.)	"	Letter from ch. in Concord, N. H.		
1082	Mary Elizabeth (Tolles) Faxon (Jas. D.)	Sept. 1, 1867	Profession of Faith.	May 0, 1869	Dis.to Plymouth ch. Lawrence, K
1083	Abby Lucretia (Harlow) Burpee (Warren L.)	"	"		
1084	Mary Ann (Worley) (Wood) (Thos. J.) Kenyon (S. P.)	"	"		
1085	Enoch Warren Wetherbee	"			
1086	Lydia D. (Field) Harvey (Daniel D.)	"	Letter from ch. in Springfield,Ms.	Feb. 28, 1869	Dis.to S.Cong.ch.Springfield,Ms.
1087	Cynthia R. (Taylor) Hayden (Charles)	"	Letter from ch. W. Lebanon, N. H.		
1088	Tamson (Ingalls) Knowlton (John O.)	"	Letter from Bap. ch. Ludlow.	Sept, 24, 1867	By death, aged 26 years.
1089	Betsey (Mitchell)(Higgins)(Moses) Cushing (Daniel)	Nov. 3, 1867	Letter f. M. E ch. Birmingham.		
1090	Mary (Lynde) Foster (Samuel)	"	Letter f. ch. San Francisco, Cal.	Jan. 24, 1869	Dis. to Pr. ch. San Francisco,Cal.
1091	Charles E. Richardson	"	Letter f. Olive St.ch.Nashua,N.H.		
1092	Granville Knight (Dr.)	"	Letter from ch. in Walpole, N. H.		
1093	Addie Herrick (Fay) Knight (Dr. Granville)	"			
1094	George O. Henry	"	Letter from ch. in Bellows Falls.		
1095	Frances A. (Howard) Henry (George O.)	"			
1096	Luella Dart	"	Profession of Faith.		
1097	Fred Barnes	"			
1098	Rhoda Ann (Whitney) Smart (Joseph)	"	"		
1099	Marcia C. (Earle) Messenger (John W.)	"	"		
1100	Merrill L. Lawrence	"			
1101	Katie L. (Locke) Lawrence (Merrill L.)	Jan. 5, 1868	Letter from M. E. ch. Lima, N. Y.		
1102	Sarah A. (Wyman) Lewis (Henry)	"	"		
1103	Marcella D. (Leland) Jenkins (Thomas L.)	"	Letter from John St.ch.Lowell,Ms		
1104	Eliza (Prentiss) Locke (Henry)	"	Letter from ch. in Grafton.		
1105	Almira F. Locke	"	Letter from ch. in Rockingham.		
1106	Jones Grimes	"	Letter from ch. in Bellows Falls.		
1107	Joseph Smart	"	Profession of Faith.		
1108	Charles Edward Doubleday	"	"		
1109	Marshall Hancock	"	"		
1110	Harriet N. (Worley) Hancock (Marshall)	"	"		
1111	Sarah (Ball) Bigelow (Barney)	"	"		
1112	Eliza (Holman) Harlow (Henry P.)	"	Letter from Bap.ch. N.Springfield.		
1113	Nancy Ann (Rogers) Barney (Franklin)	"	Profession of Faith.		
1114	Abby (Goodenow) Britton (Rodney)	"	"		
1115	Sarah Abbie (Washburn) Parker (Henry)	"	"		
1116	Lydia Putnam	"	"		
1117	Almira Harrington	"	"		
1118	Hattie Seymour Steele	"	"		

No.	Name.	Date of Recep'n.	Manner of Reception.	Date of Removal.	Manner of Removal.
1119	Abbie Woodbury	Jan. 5, 1868	Profession of Faith.		
1120	Marion G. (Franklin) Holbrook (Frank H.)	"	"		
1121	Almira (Harlow) Chipman (James)	"	"		
1122	Marvin Davis Bishee	March 1, 1868	Letter from ch. in Meriden, N. H.		
1123	Lewis Jackman	"	Letter from ch. in Weathersfield.		
1124	Ellen (Marcy) Jackman (Lewis)	"	"		
1125	Mary M. (Bronson) Pierce (Lewis A.)	"	Letter from ch.in Weatherafield E.		
1126	Sarah (Page) Spencer (Mark)	"	Letter from ch. in Westminster E.		
1127	Henry Martyn Arms	"	Profession of Faith.		
1128	Sarah Jane (Closson) Arms (Henry M.)	"	"		
1129	Warren Lorenzo Burjice	"	"		
1130	Mattie M. (Beckley) Brown (Valentine)	"	"		
1131	Julia A. (Gould) (Putnam) (Oliver) Brown (Elisha)	"	"		
1132	Gershom Lyman Closson	"	"		
1133	Edward Noble Davis	"	"		
1134	Alice Rebecca Damon	"	"		
1135	Maria Linn (Stearns) Goodenow (Henry)	"	"		
1136	Harriet E. (Burgess) Goodenow (Elhanan W.)	"	"		
1137	Carrie P.(Hasham) Randall (Eugene)	"	"		
1138	Charles Melvin Keyes	"	"		
1139	Mary Louisa (Buck) Keyes (Chas. L.)	"	"		
1140	Mary Annis Keyes	"	"		
1141	William Henry Minot	"	"		
1142	Jobiel Weston Putnam	"	"		
1143	Mariette Putnam	"	"		
1144	Ezra Alzaman Robinson	"	"		
1145	Ellen (Herrick) Robinson (Ezra A.)	"	"		
1146	Langdon Sawyer (Dr.)	"	"		
1147	Wesley Walker	"	"		
1148	Mary Elizabeth Wilson	"	"		
1149	David Aaron Wilder	"	"		
1150	Lucy Jane (Imlett) Wilder (David A.)	"	"		
1151	Frank Ezra Woodward	"	"		
1152	Marianna (Damon) Woolward (Frank E.)	May 3, 1868	"		
1153	Sarah I. (McAlister) Bailey (Aldrich A.)	"	"		
1154	William Lovell Dodge (Dr.)	"	"		
1155	Sarah Maria (Beckley) Chipman (John N.)	"	"	March 21, 1869	D. to Rollstonech.Fitchburg,Ma
1156	Mary Ella Goodenow	"	"		

No.	Name	Date	Manner	Date removed	Remarks
1157	Horace Damon Gould	"		Jan. 4, 1869	By death, aged 29 years.
1158	Eliza Burke Hall	"			
1159	Sophia Ursula (Spencer) Lewis (Wm.)	"			
1160	Zimri Messenger	"			
1161	Rosa Rhien	"			
1162	Harriet Ann (Rice) Choate (Benj. B.)	"			
1163	Alice Maria Steele	"			
1164	Nellie Maria (Eddy) Taylor (Geo. W.)	"			
1165	Ervin Alstyne Townsend	"			
1166	William Westney	"			
1167	Emma A. (Hutchins) Doubleday (Wm. O.)	"	Letter from ch. in Pittaford.		
1168	Otto Monroe Doubleday	"	"		
1169	Lydia (Tucker) Hull (Thomas)	"	Letter from ch. in Woodstock.		
1170	Charles Coolidge Johnson	"	Lttr fr.lr.ch.in Ridgeway, Minn.		
1171	Susan S. (Ellison) Johnson (Chas. C.)	"	Letter from ch. in Chester.		
1172	Sarah M. (Locke) Warren (James T.)	"	"		
1173	Russel Horrick	July 5, 1868	Letter from ch. in Malone, N. Y.	Aug. 26, 1868	By death, aged 70 years.
1174	Maria (Tyler) Herrick (Russell)	"	Letter from ch. in Perkinsville.		
1175	Huldah (Selden) Thomson (Menzies A.)	"	Letter from ch. in Madison, Wis.		
1176	Harriet Elizabeth Thomson	"	Letter from ch. Charlestown,N.H.		
1177	Orrin Putnam	"	Profession of Faith.		
1178	John Orlando Knowlton	"	"		
1179	Mary C. (Cagley) Knowlton (John O.)	"	"		
1180	Marcia Tower Aldrich	"	"		
1181	Ellen Augusta (Bisbee) Parker (James M.)	"	"		
1182	Sarah Frances Booth	"	"		
1183	Lucian Gould	"	"		
1184	Rosa Thankful Howe	"	"		
1185	Frances Ann Steele	"	"		
1186	Ellen Lucy Steele	Sept. 29, 1868	"		
1187	Abby Keyes Goddard	Nov. 1, 1868	Letter from ch. in Norwich.		
1188	Laura Janette (Parks) Harlow (Hermon W.)	"	Profession of Faith.		
1189	Cornelia Ann (Preston) Doubleday (Chas. E.)	"	"		
1190	Charles Ebenezer Hill	"	"		
1191	Horace Messenger	Jan. 10, 1869	"		
1192	Loretto L. (Houghton) Messenger (Horace)	"	"		
1193	Peres Whitcomb	"	"		
1194	Mary S. (Bates) Whitcomb (Peres)	"	"		
1195	Emeline R. (Balch)(Heath)(Reuben) Whitcomb (Lincoln)	"	"		
1196	Betsey (Tuttle) Roby (S. Allen)	"	"		
1197	Lucy Maria Chase	"	"		
1198	Lyman Whitcomb	"	"		
1199	Angelia (Kidder) Whitcomb (Lyman)	"	Letter from ch. in Townshend.		

No.	Name.	Date of Recept'n.	Manner of Reception.	Date of Removal.	Manner of Removal.
1200	Charles Proctor Bailey	March 7, 1869	Profession of Faith.		
1201	William Rufus Nutting	"	"		
1202	Mary Jane Pearson		"		
1203	Edmund Collins Nason	May 2, 1869	"		
1204	Davis Brainard Prentiss	"	"		
1205	Fanny Jane (McNab) Prentiss (Davis B.)	"	"		
1206	Helen Preston	"	"		
1207	Elbridge Gerry Ruggles	"	Letter from ch. in Marengo, Ill.		
1208	Charles Daniel Walker	"	Letter from ch. in Bridport.		
1209	Mary Ellen Woodbury	"	Letter from ch. in Peacham.		
1210	Minnie C. (Miner) Orton (John)	"	Letter from ch. in Chester.		
1211	Mary (Wood) Searle (Charles P.)	"	Letter from M. E.ch.in Springfield.		
1212	Henry H. Shaw	"	Letter from ch.in So.Londonderry.		
1213	Lucy Jane (Whiting) Shaw (Henry H.)	"	Letter from ch. Charlestown, N.H.		
1214	Thomas Marble Merritt	"	Letter from ch. in Claremont, N.H.		
1215	Emma S. (Stearns) Merritt (Thomas M.)	July 4, 1869	Letter from ch. in Windsor.		
1216	Lizzie J. (Leavitt) Brock (James)	"	Profession of Faith.		
1217	Autentia Leonard	"	"		
1218	Annette C. (Tenney) Weld (Chester)	"	"		
1219	Eliza Ann Perry	"	"		
1220	Emma Clark Hall	"	"		
1221	Frances Augusta Hall	"	"		
1222	Rufus Orestes Forbush	"	"		
1223	Daniel Locke	"	"		
1224	Lucy Gibson Gould	"	"		
1225	Eliza A. (Spencer) Forbush (R. O.)	"	"		
1226	James E. Hall				

ALPHABETICAL INDEX

OF

NAMES OF PAST MEMBERS.

	ABBOTT
234	Phebe
	ADAMS
675	Eliza M.
	AIKEN
708	Charles
709	Adeline
	ALDRICH
548	Mary T.
921	Hannah
1070	Merrill N.
1180	Marcia T.
	ALEXANDER
987	Henry W.
	ALVORD
743	Eliza J.
	AMES
211	Abigail
271	Eli
272	Nancy
	ANDREWS
1008	Semantha W.
	ANTHONY
513	Edmund P.
927	Edward P.
	ARMS
915	Rev. Selah R.
916	Mrs. Eliza (916)
917	Maria P. (1077)
957	Emily M.
985	Eliza
1127	Henry M.
1128	Sarah J.
	ATHERTON
889	Elizabeth
	ATKINSON
357	Nancy
	BAILEY
346	Mary
1153	Sarah I.
1200	Charles P.
	BAKER
911	Mary M.
	BANCROFT
474	Merrill
	BARNARD
8	Abigail
31	Lucy
253	Mary
285	John J. (904)

393	George
437	Frederic
484	Susan L.
639	Eliza
702	Solon
704	Frederic G.
720	Jenison
995	Thirza
	BARNES
497	Polly
1097	Fred
	BARNEY
1113	Nancy A.
	BARRETT
12	John
29	Betsey
288	Elizabeth
292	Mary
1078	Sybil
	BASCOM
18	Elihu
	BATES
63	Esther
72	Dea. Phinehas
73	Abigail
141	Huldah
202	Ruth
255	Allen (691)
256	Anna (692)
265	Rachel (942)
299	Theophilus
757	Catharine S.
767	Nancy
839	Sarah M.
968	Emily V.
	BEELS
90	Abigail
	BELKNAP
187	Sarah
290	Lydia
845	Phebe F.
	BELLOWS
77	James
471	Lucy
	BEMIS
39	Lucy
	BENNETT
772	Gratia A.
	BIGELOW
1111	Sarah

	BINGHAM
610	Prudence
	BISBEE
34	Abner jr.
35	Barbara
50	Mary
95	Elisha
96	Mary
132	Nancy
204	John
312	John B.
345	Arethusa
455	Elijah
462	Hiram
463	Betsey
526	Abner A.
527	Martha A.
534	Abner
535	Cynthia
1122	Marvin D.
	BIXBY
19	Adonijah
20	Mary
198	Abigail
206	Moses
	BLANCHARD
55	Polly
384	Stephen
385	Rebecca
562	Mary
753	Mary A.
	BOOTH.
1054	Caroline F.
1059	James
1060	Marion E.
1080	Edward A.
1182	Sarah F.
	BOURNE
3	Dea. Newcomb
4	Abigail
183	Daniel
184	Abigail
316	Dea. Abraham J.
550	William T.
	BOWEN
579	Lorinda
1017	James C.
1018	Mary E.
	BOWERS
1032	Dr. George

500	Parkman jr.
301	Chauncey
302	Tural B.
307	Mary
438	Ira
490	Mary
518	Isaac G.
561	Martha J.
583	Lydia
676	William
677	Amelia M. (796)
714	Mary A.
782	Harriet A.
794	Betsey
795	Elvira
812	Albert
840	Eliza
853	Maria
883	Mary K.
941	Sarah
977	Lucia A.
1133	Edward N.

DAVIDSON
230	Hannah (1012)
293	John
294	Abigail
397	James
1011	Dea. William

DAY
418	Abby
522	Mary

DEAN
570	Artemas

DEMARY
476	Jane

DERBY
774	Lucretia
775	Mary A.
828	Samuel
864	Harriet M.
971	Elizabeth F.
1057	Olive A.

DICKINSON
950	William

DINSMORE
694	James
695	Zilpha
698	Rebecca
846	Tryphene

DODGE
319	William
320	Abigail
464	William
515	Christopher
731	Hosea W.
732	Lyman
1154	Dr. William L.

DOUBLEDAY
1108	Charles E,
1167	Emma A.
1168	Otto M.
1189	Cornelia A.

DOWNS
793	Sophronia P.

DRAPER
9	Sarah

DUNKLEE
1049	Mary J.

DURREN
647	Sarah M.

DURRENT
268	Susanna
321	Theoda
359	Luther

369	Joseph
370	Sarah
372	Calvin (593)
496	Emeline S.
495	Susanna

DUTTON
756	Rebecca

DYER
305	Fanny

DYKE
607	Samuel

EARLS
631	Halford
897	Mary B.

EATON
93	Joshua
94	Rebecca
632	Deborah
798	John P.
802	Asa
831	Emily J.

EDGELL
124	Mary G.

EDSON
773	Clementine
841	Laura

ELLIS
377	Abigail
456	Jacob
785	Jeremiah
786	Hannah
825	Joseph W.
961	Isaac
962	Mary A.
972	Julia F.

ELLISON
327	Mary A.

EVANS
13	Asher
165	Phila.

FAIRBANKS
173	Moses
679	Nancy
849	Sarah E.

FARNSWORTH
736	Charles
737	Louisa

FARRAR
69	Lydia
859	Caroline

FAXON
1082	Mary E.

FELLOWS
858	Emily S.

FELT
955	Elvira

FIELD
98	Jerusha
871	Susan
880	Marcia
1055	Louisa

FISHER
148	Orathy
193	Jacob
194	Clarissa
663	Harriet

FISKE
1068	Juliette H.
904	Arabel

FLETCHER
787	George W.

FLING
472	Belinda
498	William E.
499	Sarah

FLOYD
342	Anna

FORDUSH
923	Elizabeth
1222	R. Orestes
1225	Eliza A.

FOSTER
1090	Mary

FRANCE
758	Orinda E.
799	Hermon E.

FULLAM
1004	Mary M.

FURBER
608	Dr. Z. W.
609	Caroline

GEAR
630	John

GIDDINGS
940	Mary E.

GILKEY
104	Dea. Walter R.

GILL
164	Thankful
243	Theoda
602	Mary

GILSON
54	Eunice
907	Sarah
958	Eunice
1007	Anna

GLYNN
740	Lucy T.

GODDARD
928	Nelson W.
929	Sarah D.
956	Fanny
1051	Ariel E.
1187	Abby K.

GOODENOW
54	Eunice
686	Lucy B.
811	Elhanan W.
1135	Maria L.
1136	Harriet F.
1156	Mary Ella

GOODMAN
291	Nancy B.

GOULD
88	Theodocia
925	Hannah
1157	Horace D.
1183	Lucian
1224	Lucy G.

GRAHAM
355	Rebecca
816	Dana

GREELEY
585	John

GRIMES
685	Sophia
830	Matilda A.
906	James A
1106	Jones

GRINNELL
550	Sarah T.
746	Marcia
768	Abel H.
1058	Sarah C.

GRISWOLD
45	Betsey
368	Daniel

GROUT
488	Lydia
683	Dea. Alexander

684	Esther	160	John		**HYDE**
747	Esther	161	Esther	329	Jane
754	Nancy F.		**HEATON**		**INGHAM**
827	Daniel A.	614	Fanny	1079	Edward
857	William K.	615	Keziah		**JACKMAN**
855	Nancy J.	616	Nancy	1123	Lewis
	GUILD		**HENCHEY**	1124	Ellen
890	Maria	960	Margaret		**JAMESON**
	HALL		**HENRY**	1019	Rev. Thomas
481	Louisa	569	Hyren		**JASEPH**
622	Atalanta	1094	George O.	580	Mary
665	John	1095	Frances A.		**JENKINS**
761	Augusta A.		**HERRICK**	507	George
804	Edward	1173	Russell	508	Merrill
926	Frances O.	1174	Maria	820	Thomas L.
1025	Abby L.		**HILDRETH**	1103	Marcella D.
1050	Mary A.	247	Anna		**JEWETT**
1069	George R.		**HILL**	275	Susanna S.
1158	Eliza B.	807	Samuel D.		**JOHNSON**
1169	Lydia	848	Eliza A.	311	Alexander H.
1220	Emma C.	1190	Charles E.	334	Betsey
1221	Frances A.		**HODGES**	473	Elizabeth S.
1226	James E.	411	Mary S.	540	Sarah
	HANCOCK		**HOLBROOK**	549	Solomon
1109	Marshall	1120	Mariou G.	599	George
1110	Harriet N.		**HOLDEN**	729	Chester W.
	HARDY	62	Deborah	730	Louisa M.
110	Clarissa	413	Submit D.	1170	Charles C.
	HARLOW	529	John	1171	Susan S.
308	Wells	591	Nathaniel		**JONES**
875	Lewis W.	592	Hannah	111	Ann
876	Laura	717	Martha A.	348	Louisa
1112	Eliza	847	Nancy	523	Elizabeth
1188	Nettie L.	967	Jane M.	760	Gratia L.
	HARRINGTON	969	Elizabeth		**KANOW**
421	Leonard	970	Harriet E.	80	Elizabeth
572	Rosabelle	993	William M.		**KEMP**
1117	Almira		**HOLMAN**	701	George S.
	HARRIS	267	Sally		**KENDALL**
282	Mercy	296	Dea. Arba	783	Cynthia A.
	HARVEY	297	Hannah		**KENNEY**
1086	Lydia D.	924	Sophia	415	Sarah
	HASKELL	976	Mary		**KENTON**
215	Roxana	543	Smith	1084	Mary A.
216	Content		**HOLMES**		**KEYES**
689	Abigail	642	Harriet	423	Lucia
	HASKINS		**HOUSE**	444	Franklin
166	Rhoda	276	Nancy	1138	Charles M.
	HATCH	516	David	1139	Mary L.
133	Hannah		**HOWARD**	1140	Mary A.
	HAWKINS	68	Azubah		**KING**
176	Dea. Horatio G. (935)		**HOWE**	744	Thankful
171	Polly	1184	Rosa T.		**KITCHELL**
244	Louisa	741	Martha	936	Francis
349	Horatio B.		**HUDDARD**		**KNAPP**
350	Abigail	65	Sarah	721	Richard
553	Sarah	81	Anna	722	Rhoda A.
	HAYDEN	101	Calvin		**KNIGHT**
191	Mary	102	Anna	836	Bethiah
1087	Cynthia R.	123	Horace	893	Dr. E. A.
	HAYWOOD	207	Lemuel S.	894	Mary
129	Catharine	401	Ruth	1092	Dr. Granville
443	Mary A.	539	Ruth	1093	Addie H.
564	Martha J.	612	Harriet		**KNOWLTON**
666	Dea.George P.	613	Nancy	1088	Tamson
705	Mary	617	Ann E.	1178	John O.
738	David H.	635	Laura	1179	Mary C.
818	Samuel	662	Elizabeth		**LABAREE**
819	James	699	Dr. Calvin	82	Joseph
980	Catharine R.	978	Elizabeth H.		**LAKE**
1001	Dea. Charles		**HUNTER**	445	Enoch
1002	Parthena	810	George	446	Charlotte
	HEALD		**HURD**		**LANE**
64	Polly	367	Lydia	239	Susan
151	Lydia				

	LANSING
966	Joseph
	LAWRENCE
1045	Merrill L. (1100)
1101	Katie L.
	LEACH
190	Phinetta
	LEETE
248	Sarah
	LELAND
625	Martha
	LEONARD
1217	Autentia
	LEWIS
260	Nancy
284	Dea. Isaac M.
645	Leura
835	Lucia W.
1022	Minerva E.
1102	Sarah A.
1159	Sophia G.
333	Maria
	LISCOMB
884	Aurelia S.
885	Esther A.
	LITCHFIELD
287	Eunice
742	Lucy
959	Mary S.
1071	Abigail S.
	LOCKE
266	Lucy
587	Nancy (984)
596	Daniel (1223)
597	Elethia
983	Dea. Orin
1043	Nelson W.
1047	Olive L.
1065	Hattie N.
1104	Eliza
1105	Almira F.
	LOCKWOOD
431	Seymour
432	Lucy
	LORD
493	Elvira
	LOVELAND
943	Dorilla
953	Lizzie B.
1013	John C.
	LOVELL
232	Mary
251	Mary
354	Lucretia O. (919)
428	Don
563	Abigail J.
918	James
948	Almera
	LULL
764	Mary L.
	LYNDE
107	Hannah
	MANN
257	Silence
	MANSON
745	Betsey S.
	MARBLE
860	Jane
	MARTIN
379	Betsey
	MASON
393	Elmira
	MATHER
107	Lydia

	McCLENITHAN
690	Mary E.
	McDONALD
1076	Elizabeth B.
	McCORMICK
1031	Abigail
	MEACHAM
937	Eliza J.
	MEADE
138	Eli
139	Sarah
	MEEKS
224	John
	MERRITT
117	Clementine
920	Thomas M. (1214)
1215	Emma S.
	MESSER
531	Joseph
532	Mary
	MESSENGER
867	William M.
868	Arabella S.
1036	Rachel J.
1099	Marcia C.
1160	Zimri
1191	Horace
1192	Lorette L.
	MILES.
626	Abel
627	Elizabeth
	MILLER
114	Sophia
387	Statira
600	Susan
777	John
	MINOT
362	Electa F.
844	Louisa
1141	William H.
	MITCHELL
719	Mary
878	Betsey
	MONTAGUE
318	Betsey
	MOORE
759	Lucina
975	Laura J.
	MORTON
390	Rev. D. O.
361	Lucretia
362	Electa F.
606	Levi P.
	MUDGETT
1037	Sarah J.
	MUNN
901	Calvin
902	Mehitable
	MUNSELL
577	Cynthia
628	Cynthia
629	Mary
	MURFEE
748	Sophia W.
	NASH
510	Elzabeth
	NASON
1203	Edmund C.
	NEWTON
1025	Elizabeth F.
	NICHOLS
26	Levi
27	Elizabeth
42	Dea. David
43	Naomi

186	Sarah
258	Pamelia
408	Francis K.
409	Frances
457	Hiram H.
458	Pamelia
	NOBLE
712	Emeline
	NOURSE
108	Martha
157	Peter
158	Martha
323	Zilpha
406	Martha M.
604	Peter U.
578	Marcia M.
1046	Hattie J.
	NYE
44	Lucretia
	NUTTING
1201	William R.
	OAKES
140	Elizabeth
182	Nancy
	OLNEY
240	Elsa
371	Welcome
752	Eliza
	ONION
210	Jemima
	ORTON
1210	Minnie C.
	PAGE
330	Phebe
	PARKER
475	Lucia
560	Sarah
1010	Henry J.
1115	Sarah A.
1181	Ellen A.
	PARKS
246	Betsey
295	Frederic
378	Elvira
	PARNELL
715	Benjamin (898)
716	Mary (899)
	PEARSON
1202	Mary J.
	PEASE
113	Eunice
	PERRY
259	Sally
1219	Eliza A.
	PERSONS
87	Lydia
92	Oliver
	PETTINGILL
487	Sally
1023	Elizabeth
	PIERCE
203	Rispa B.
217	Ruth
386	Louisa
390	Nathaniel
391	Anna
503	William
552	Adeline
619	Lucius M.
1024	Leroy M.
1125	Mary M.
	PINGRY
389	Lucy G.
	PLACE
127	Eleanor

	POMEROY	900	Maria P.	162	Betsey
430	Jacob		RICHARDS		SHAW
519	Don A.	277	Perrin N.	873	Orinda
586	Sophia	278	Emily	930	Salina M.
	PORTER		RICHARDSON	1212	Henry H.
331	Hannah	485	Nancy	1213	Lucy J.
465	Fanny	1091	Charles E.		SHEDD
525	Frederic A.		RICHMOND	156	Lydia
728	Mark R.	672	Amaziah	172	Elizabeth
749	Lucretia	673	Harriet	181	Elizabeth
792	Lydia A.		RIDGEWAY		SHERWIN
821	Charles E.	335	Emily	912	Maria
973	Harriet A.		ROBINSON		SLACK
	POWELL	263	Lydia	1015	John A.
260	Jane	850	Nancy E.		SMART
	POWERS	1144	Ezra A.	1098	Rhoda A.
274	Sally	1145	Ellen	1107	Joseph
439	George C.		ROBY		SMILEY
	PRATT	1196	Betsey	22	Rev. Robinson
86	Deborah		ROGERS	25	Elizabeth
119	Daniel	226	Ephraim	70	David
462	Catharine	252	Elizabeth	71	Mary
584	Thomas M.	403	Jonathan	317	Nancy
598	George		ROSS	678	Sarah
682	Daniel B.	174	Jane	700	Thomas H.
750	Rosanna		RUGGLES	806	David R.
751	Eliza A.	1207	Elbridge G.		SMITH
	PRENTISS		RUMRILL	15	Isaac
336	Hannah	651	Sarah A.	38	Betsey
356	Henry jr.		SABIN	59	Mary
620	Henry	931	Charles	269	Ruth
621	Mary	932	Abby	414	Joseph
1204	Davis B.		SAFFORD	466	Daniel
1205	Fanny J	264	Nancy (N)	467	Lucia
	PRESTON	427	Noah	505	Jerusha
1206	Helen	479	Lucretia P.	551	Jesse M.
	PRIEST	776	Nancy (H)	559	Abigail
89	Sarah	824	Henry	637	John C.
	PROCTOR	988	Almira	638	Abby
238	Sarah	1067	Abby	643	Elizabeth
279	Sarah		SARGENT	659	Chauncey H.
	PROUTY	809	James L.	724	Daniel
771	Martha		SARTWELL	905	Lucy M.
	PUTNAM	32	Oliver	757	Catharine G.
189	Sarah	33	Hannah		SNELL
315	Asahel	57	Eleazer	574	Sally
477	Harriet	58	Hannah	657	Leverett M
478	Cynthia		SAWYER		SNOWDEN
636	Emily	352	Sarah J.	1027	Lydia A.
801	Timothy	671	Marcia		SPALDING
1116	Lydia	679	Sarah	991	Maria R.
1142	Jehiel W.	1075	Sarah		SPENCER
1143	Mariette	1146	Dr. Langdon	11	Simeon
1177	Orrin		SCOFIELD	37	Mercy
	RANDALL	227	Luke	409	Eliza A.
40	Eunice		SCOTT	410	Abigail
201	Nancy	56	Samuel	494	Sarah
373	Smith		SEARLE	517	Jonas B.
1137	Carrie P.	1211	Mary	546	Ellen M.
	REED		SELDEN	571	Amelia (908)
152	Joseph	130	Dea. Joseph	650	Betsey
153	Mary	131	Huldah	822	James
154	Leafy	223	Joseph Jr. (652)	862	Susan
	REYNOLDS	245	Olive (653)	1126	Sarah
634	Catharine	298	Rev. Calvin		SPRING
	RHIEU	542	Eliza	788	Zeno E.
1161	Rosa		SHAEFFER	789	Arvilla
	RICE	680	Harriet N.	854	Lydia
17	David	974	Eleanor P.		STEARNS
52	Sally		SHATTUCK	1056	Mary
486	Sarah	60	Samuel		STEELE
530	Timothy W.	61	Hannah	159	Sophia
590	Susan	121	Weston	219	Helenery
725	Charles H.	122	Hartwell	228	Dea. Ashbel (933)
829	Lois	144	Mercy	229	Ann

326	Lucy M. (934)	514	Martha	1066	Anna E.	
483	Elizabeth		TOWER		WATKINS	
594	Samuel Jr. (998)	16	Betsey	952	G. Augustus	
595	Sophia	21	Elizabeth	1000	Elizabeth T.	
944	Electa	163	Elizabeth		WEBSTER	
999	Mary C.	339	Esther	306	Ireno	
1118	Hattie S.	343	Sally		WEEKS	
1163	Alice M.	451	Isaac	1006	Ebenezer T.	
1185	Frances A.	452	Susanna		WELD	
1186	Ellen L.	470	Bethiah	1218	Annette C.	
	STEVENS	511	Caroline		WEST	
5	Simon	573	Nancy L.	400	Lydia	
36	Catharine	733	Stoddard		WESTNEY	
195	Mary A.	850	Tila O.	1166	William	
196	Fanny	946	Laura		WETHERBEE	
262	John 2d	982	Mary N.	1085	Enoch W.	
309	Adeline		TOWN		WHEELER	
436	Simon	155	Lois	109	Sarah	
492	Mary A.	1052	Charles	990	Harriet	
529	Silsby	1053	Susan S.		WHEELOCK	
558	Caroline M.		TOWNSEND	855	Sarah J.	
603	Albert	1029	Frederic V. A.		WHIPPLE	
604	Alfred	1030	Amelia	214	Martha	
605	George	1165	Ervin A.	313	Sally	
611	Talitha		TYRRELL	322	Sybil	
	STIMSON	422	Abigail R.	324	Sabrina	
554	Ann	668	Hiram	461	Ormus M.	
	STREETER	669	Mary A.	688	James B.	
392	Susanna	834	Mary A.	843	Mary A.	
	STURTEVANT	1016	Rhoda J.		WHITCOMB	
640	Elisha		UNDERHILL	28	Priscilla	
641	Mary	383	Persis H.	97	Anna	
	SWIFT		UNDERWOOD	176	Shubael	
382	Christina	142	Eunice	177	Ruth	
863	Phebe		UPHAM	236	Catharine	
949	Frances	1048	Sarah L.	303	Delight B.	
	TAFT		VAUGHAN	314	Lucretia	
869	Daniel	997	Elizabeth L.	337	Polly	
870	Sophronia		WALES	351	Israel	
	TAYLOR	399	Eunice	394	Jacob	
199	Charlotte		WALKER	395	Salmon (895)	
442	Noah C.	14	Hannah	396	Fanny (896)	
861	Julia F.	135	Martha	491	Phebe	
891	Rev. Lathrop	366	Almira L.	649	DeWitt C.	
892	Hannah T.	374	Mary	664	Mary S.	
989	Sarah	388	Priscilla	687	Abraham	
1164	Nellie M.	449	James	781	Lucia M.	
	TENNEY	450	Mary	784	Lincoln	
218	Edna (996)	565	Ephraim	826	Arthur C.	
405	Mary A.	589	Tryphenia	838	Sarah J.	
417	Willard	623	Jemima	1193	Peres	
1014	John G.	815	James L.	1194	Mary S.	
1081	Rev. Samuel G.	965	William	1195	Emeline R.	
	THAYER	1040	Lizzie A.	1198	Lyman	
567	Charles L.	1147	Wesley	1199	Angelia	
568	Mary A.	1208	Charles D.		WHITE	
	THOMPSON		WARD	180	John	
84	Betsey	41	Naamah	192	Rev. Seneca	
425	Aaron L.	851	Martha W.	212	Rev. Joseph B.	
537	Ann	881	Louisa T.	225	Peter	
648	John S.		WARDNER	696	Bethiah	
1003	Horace W.	837	Sarah E.	879	Calvin S.	
	THOMSON		WARREN	979	Harriet L.	
205	James B.	654	Joseph		WHITING	
420	Sally B.	655	Jesse	797	Joseph	
1175	Huldah	656	Betsey	833	Mary W.	
1176	Harriet E.	1172	Sarah M.	842	Lucy A.	
	THORNTON		WASHBURN	872	Clarissa	
118	Rosetta M.	105	Rev. Ebenezer		WHITMAN	
800	Charles C.	125	Ebenezer	208	Abram	
865	Tryphena M.	126	Abigail		WHITMORE	
	THURSTON	188	Achsah	433	Hamlin	
624	Nancy	250	Harriet		WHITNEY	
	TOLLES	790	David W.	1	Dea. Lemuel	
61	Miriam	1038	Mary R.	2	Thankful	

116	Susanna		**WILSON**	734	George
222	Dea. Elijah	48	John	735	Mary A.
328	Mary R.	49	Barbara	992	George B.
512	Norman K.	710	Gardner	1064	Joseph
713	Hannah	711	Martha A.	1072	Frances A.
857	Mary J.	1148	Mary E.	1119	Abbie
	WICKER		**WISE**	1209	Mary Ellen
633	Susanna	231	Harriet		**WOODWARD**
	WILCOX		**WISEWALL**	53	Eunice
903	Clarissa	660	Isaac	134	Polly
	WILDER	661	Rosetta	506	Sarah
670	George M.	874	Mary A.	1151	Frank E.
1149	David A.		**WOOD**	1152	Marianna D.
1150	Lucy J.	241	Fanny		**WOOLSON**
	WILKINS	533	Hannah	524	Dea. Amasa (909)
289	Nancy	886	Relief B.	581	Mary (910)
	WILKINSON	707	Hannah C.	954	Helen A.
404	Mary C.		**WOODBURY**	1034	Mary
	WILLIAMS	168	Jonathan		**WORKS**
254	Elizabeth	169	Sally	416	Lucinda
344	Eunice	332	Elizabeth	566	John
365	Hannah	338	Betsey	575	Sarah T.
644	Lucretia	340	Elizabeth		**WRIGHT**
762	Jonathan	582	Mary	480	Harriet
763	Elizabeth	600	Sarah	813	Ephraim
852	Eunice	601	Joann	913	Mary L.
922	Henrietta E.				

NAMES

OF THE

PRESENT OFFICERS AND MEMBERS.

[* Designates non-resident Members.]

---•◆•---

PASTOR,

REV. L. H. COBB.

DEACONS:

ASHBEL STEELE,   AMASA WOOLSON,
GEORGE P. HAYWOOD,   ADNA BROWN.

CHURCH COMMITTEE:

THE PASTOR,   AMASA WOOLSON,
ASHBEL STEELE,   ADNA BROWN,
GEORGE P. HAYWOOD,   REV. S. G. TENNEY,
            HENRY CLOSSON, CLERK.

MEMBERS:

1070	Mrs. Merrill N. Aldrich,	1122	Marvin D. Bisbee,
1180	Marcia T. Aldrich,	1054	Mrs. Caroline F. Booth,
1077	Maria P. Arms,	1059	James Booth,
1127	Henry M. Arms,	1060	Mrs. Marion E. Booth,
1128	Mrs. Sarah J. Arms,	1182	Sarah F. Booth,
		1017	James C. Bowen,
1153	Mrs. Sarah I. Bailey,	1018	Mary F. Bowen,
1200	Charles P. Bailey,	1032	Dr. George Bowers,
994	John J. Barnard,	1033	Mrs. Urania E. Bowers,
995	Mrs. Thirza Barnard,	1216	Mrs. Lizzie J. Brock,
1097	Fred Barnes,*	674	David Brown,
1113	Mrs. Nancy A. Barney,	1114	Mrs. Abby Britton,
288	Elizabeth Barrett,	963	Dea. Adna Brown,
292	Mary Barrett,	1044	Mrs. Fannie Brown,
1078	Mrs. Sybil Barrett,	1130	Mrs. Mattie M. Brown,
1111	Mrs. Sarah Bigelow,	1131	Mrs. Julia A. Brown,
534	Abner Bisbee,	951	Mrs. Lydia Burbank,
535	Mrs. Cynthia Bisbee,	325	Mrs. Eliza Burke,

706	Gratia Burke,	495	Susanna Durrent,*
1129	Warren L. Burpee,		
1083	Mrs. Abby L. Burpee,	798	John P. Eaton,
1039	Mrs. Eliza A. Butterfield,	831	Mrs. Emily J. Eaton,
		773	Mrs. Clementine Edson,
235	Mrs. Mary Caldwell,	377	Mrs. Abigail Ellis,*
938	Dea. John Chase,	786	Mrs. Hannah Ellis,
939	Mrs. Lucy Chase,	962	Mary A. Ellis,
1197	Lucy Maria Chase,	972	Julia F. Ellis,*
447	John Chipman,		
448	Mrs. Gratia Chipman,	679	Mrs. Nancy Fairbanks,*
780	Gratia A. Chipman,	858	Mrs. Emily S. Fellows,*
1121	Mrs. Almira Chipman,	1055	Mrs. Louisa Field,*
1155	Mrs. Sarah M. Chipman,	880	Marcia Field,
1062	Benj. B. Choate,	904	Mrs. Arabel Fiske,*
1162	Mrs. Harriet A. Choate,	1068	Juliette H. Fiske,
555	George R. Clark,	923	Mrs. Elizabeth Forbush,
770	Judge Henry Closson,	1222	R. Orestes Forbush,
618	Mrs. Emily Closson,	1225	Mrs. Eliza A. Forbush,
823	Col. Henry W. Closson,	1004	Mrs. Mary M. Fullam,
1132	Gershom L. Closson,		
1005	Mrs. Malina W. Closson,	243	Mrs. Theoda Gill,
1073	Rev. L. Henry Cobb,	1007	Mrs. Anna Gilson,
1074	Mrs. Harriet J. Cobb,	1187	Abby K. Goddard,
882	Mrs. Hannah L. Coffin,*	1136	Mrs. Harriet E. Goodenow,
1026	Moses Coffin,	1135	Mrs. Maria L. Goodenow,
1042	Mrs. Caroline A. Coffin,	1156	Mary Ella Goodenow,
1061	Mrs. Elizabeth F. Colcord,	925	Hannah Gould
544	Selden Cook,	1224	Lucy G. Gould,
545	Mrs. Mary Cook,	1157	Horace D. Gould,
866	Mrs. Martha B. Crain,	1183	Lucian Gould,
765	Daniel Cushing,	816	Dana Graham,
1089	Mrs. Betsey Cushing,	355	Mrs. Rebecca Graham,
832	Mrs. Adeline Cutler,	1106	Jones Grimes,
1009	Mrs. Lucretia Cutler,	830	Mrs. Matilda A. Grimes,
		747	Mrs. Esther Grout,
1134	Alice R. Damon,	754	Nancy F. Grout,
1096	Luella Dart,		
1012	Mrs. Hannah Davidson,	685	John Hall,
301	Chauncy Davis,	481	Mrs. Louisa Hall,
794	Betsey Davis,	1158	Eliza B. Hall
853	Maria Davis,	804	Edward Hall,
438	Ira Davis,	761	Mrs. Augusta A. Hall,
977	Mrs. Lucia A. Davis,	1226	James E. Hall,
518	Isaac G. Davis,	1220	Emma C. Hall,
883	Mrs. Mary K. Davis,	1221	Frances A. Hall,
1133	Edward N. Davis,	1069	George R. Hall,
812	Albert Davis,	1050	Mrs. Mary A. Hall,
828	Samuel Derby,	1169	Mrs. Lydia Hall,*
1057	Mrs. Olive A. Derby,	1109	Marshall Hancock,*
846	Tryphene Dinsmore,*	1110	Mrs. Harriet N. Hancock,*
1167	Mrs. Emma A. Doubleday,	1112	Mrs. Eliza Harlow,
1108	Charles E. Doubleday,	1188	Mrs. L. Nettie Harlow,
1189	Mrs. Cornelia A. Doubleday,	1117	Almira Harrington,
1168	Otto M. Doubleday,	689	Mrs. Abigail Haskell,
1049	Mrs. Mary J. Dunklee,	244	Mrs. Louisa Hawkins,

1087	Mrs. Cynthia R. Hayden,	983	Dea. Orin Locke,
1001	Dea. Charles Haywood,	984	Mrs. Nancy Locke,
1002	Mrs. Parthena Haywood,	1065	Hattie N. Locke,
413	Mrs. Mary A. Haywood,	1043	Nelson W. Locke,
666	Dea. George P. Haywood,	1017	Mrs. Olive L. Locke,
564	Mrs. Martha J. Haywood,	1104	Mrs. Eliza Locke,
960	Mrs. Margaret Henchey,*	1105	Almira F. Locke,
1094	George O. Henry,	1223	Daniel Locke.
1095	Mrs. Frances A. Henry,	431	Seymour Lockwood,
1174	Mrs. Maria T. Herrick,	432	Mrs Lucy Lockwood,
1190	Charles E. Hill,	1013	John C. Loveland,
1120	Mrs. Marion G. Holbrook,	918	James Lovell,
993	William M. Holden,	948	Mrs. Almera Lovell,
847	Mrs. Nancy Holden,		
969	Elizabeth Holden,*	745	Mrs. Betsey S. Manson,*
970	Harriet E. Holden,*	398	Mrs. Almira Mason,
1183	Rosa T. Howe,	1214	Thomas M. Merritt,
699	Dr. Calvin Hubbard,	1215	Mrs. Emma S. Merritt,
662	Mrs. Elizabeth Hubbard,	1160	Zimri Messenger,
973	Elizabeth H. Hubbard,	1036	Mrs. Rachel J. Messenger,
810	George Hunter,*	1191	Horace Messenger,
		1192	Mrs. Lorette L. Messenger,
1079	Edward Ingham,	1099	Mrs. Marcia C. Messenger,
		531	Joseph Messer,
1123	Lewis Jackman,	532	Mrs. Mary Messer,
1124	Mrs.Ellen Jackman,	844	Mrs. Louisa Minot,*
507	George Jenkins,	1111	William H. Minot,
508	Mrs. Merrill Jenkins,	1037	Sarah J. Mudgett,
820	Thomas L. Jenkins,		
1103	Mrs. Marcella D. Jenkins,	1203	Edward C. Nason,
334	Mrs. Betsey Johnson,	1016	Mrs. Hattie J. Nourse,*
1170	Charles C. Johnson,	1201	William R. Nutting,
1171	Mrs. Susan S. Johnson,		
		371	Welcome Olney,
1084	Mrs. Mary A, Kenyon,	752	Mrs. Eliza Olney,
1138	Charles M. Keyes.	1210	Mrs. Minnie C. Orton,
1139	Mrs. Mary L. Keyes,		
1140	Mary A. Keyes,	330	Mrs. Phebe Page,
836	Mrs. Bethiah Knight,	1010	Henry J. Parker,
893	Dr. E. Adams Knight,	1115	Mrs. Sarah A. Parker,
894	Mrs, Mary Knight,	1181	Mrs. Ellen A. Parker,
1092	Dr. Granville Knight,	295	Frederic Parks,
1093	Mrs. Addie H. Knight.	378	Mrs. Elvira Parks,
1178	John O. Knowlton,	1202	Mary J. Pearson.
1179	Mrs. Mary C. Knowlton,	1219	Eliza A. Perry,
		1024	Leroy M. Pierce,
966	Joseph Lansing,	1125	Mrs. Mary M. Pierce,
1100	Merrill L. Lawrence,	331	Mrs. Hannah Porter,
1101	Mrs. Katie L. Lawrence,	749	Mrs. Lucretia Porter,
190	Mrs. Phinetta Leach,*	336	Hannah Prentiss,
1217	Autentia Leonard,	1204	Davis B. Prentiss,
333	Mrs. Maria Lewis,*	1205	Mrs. Fanny J. Prentiss,
645	Mrs. Leura Lewis,	1206	Helen Preston,
1022	Minerva E. Lewis,	279	Sarah Proctor,*
1102	Mrs. Sarah A. Lewis,	771	Martha Prouty,
1071	Mrs. Abigail S. Litchfield,	801	Timothy Putnam,
266	Mrs. Lucy Locke,		

636	Mrs. Emily Putnam,
1116	Lydia Putnam,
1142	Jehiel W. Putnam,
1143	Marriette Putnam,
1177	Orrin Putnam,
1137	Mrs. Carrie P. Randall,
1161	Rosa Rhieu,
900	Mrs. Maria P. Rice,
1091	Charles E. Richardson,
1144	Ezra A. Robinson,
1145	Mrs. Ellen Robinson,
1196	Mrs. Betsey Roby,
174	Mrs. Jane Ross, *
1207	Elbridge G. Ruggles,
824	Henry Safford,
1067	Mrs. Abby Safford,
988	Mrs. Almira Safford,
1146	Dr. Langdon Sawyer,
1075	Mrs. Sarah Sawyer,
1211	Mrs. Mary Searle,
298	Rev. Calvin Selden,*
542	Eliza Selden,
974	Mrs. Eleanor P.Shaeffer,*
930	Salina Maria Shaw,
1212	Prof. Henry H. Shaw,
1213	Mrs. Lucy J. Shaw,
1107	Joseph Smart,
1098	Mrs. Rhoda A. Smart,
414	Joseph Smith,
637	John C. Smith,*
905	Mrs. Lucy M. Smith,*
574	Mrs Sally Snell.
1126	Mrs. Sarah Spencer,
1056	Mrs. Mary Stearns,*
228	Dea. Ashbel Steele, (933)
944	Mrs. Electa Steele,
1186	Ellen L. Steele,
1118	Hattie S. Steele,
1185	Frances A. Steele,
1163	Alice M. Steele,
219	Helenery Steele,
998	Samuel Steele, Jr.
999	Mrs. Mary C. Steele,
863	Mrs. Phebe Swift,
861	Mrs. Julia F, Taylor,
989	Mrs. Sarah Taylor,
1164	Mrs. Nellie M. Taylor,
1081	Rev. Samuel G. Tenney,
996	Mrs Edna Tenney
1014	John G. Tenney,
1003	Horace W. Thompson,
420	Sally B. Thomson,
1175	Mrs. Huldah Thomson,

1176	Hattie E. Thomson,
118	Mrs. Rosetta M. Thornton
850	Mrs. Tila O. Tower,
946	Mrs. Laura Tower,
1029	Frederick V. A. Townsend
1030	Mrs Amelia Townsend,
1165	Ervin A. Townsend,
669	Mrs. Mary A. Tyrrell,
450	Mrs. Mary Walker,
965	William Walker,
1040	Mrs. Lizzie A. Walker,
1147	Wesley Walker,
1208	Charles D. Walker.
837	Mrs. Sarah E. Wardner,
1172	Mrs. Sarah M. Warren,
188	Mrs. Achsah Washburn,
1038	Mrs. Mary R. Washburn,
1066	Mrs. Anna E. Washburn,
1006	Ebenezer T. Weeks,*
1218	Mrs Annette C. Weld,
1166	William Westney,
1085	Enoch W. Wetherbee,
990	Mrs. Harriet Wheeler,
322	Mrs Sybil Whipple,
688	James B. Whipple,
843	Mrs. Mary A. Whipple,
236	Mrs. Catharine Whitcomb,
303	Mrs. Delight B. Whitcomb,
351	Israel Whitcomb,
491	Mrs. Phebe Whitcomb,
664	Mrs. Mary S. Whitcomb,
781	Mrs. Lucia M. Whitcomb,
784	Lincoln Whitcomb,
1195	Mrs. Emeline R. Whitcomb,
1193	Perez Whitcomb,
1194	Mrs. Mary S. Whitcomb,
1198	Lyman Whitcomb,
1199	Mrs. Angelia Whitcomb,
979	Mrs. Harriet L. White
842	Mrs. Lucy A. Whiting,
514	Norman K. Whitney,*
903	Mrs. Clarissa Wilcox,*
1149	David A. Wilder,
1150	Mrs. Lucy J. Wilder,
344	Eunice Williams,*
1148	Mary E. Wilson,
660	Isaac Wisewall,
874	Mrs. Mary A. Wisewall,
582	Mary Woodbury,
600	Sarah Woodbury,
734	George Woodbury,
735	Mrs. Mary A. Woodbury,
992	George B. Woodbury,
1064	Joseph Woodbury,
1072	Frances A. Woodbury,

1119	Abbie Woodbury,	909	Dea. Amasa Woolson.
1209	Mary Ellen Woodbury,	1034	Mrs. Mary Woolson,
1151	Frank E. Woodward.*	416	Lucinda Works,*
1152	Mrs. Marianna Woodward,*	480	Harriet Wright.

———•———

WHOLE NO. OF PRESENT MEMBERS,	361
NO. OF MALE MEMBERS,	116
NO. OF FEMALE MEMBERS,	245
NO. OF NON-RESIDENT MEMBERS,	31

www.ingramcontent.com/pod-product-compliance
Lightning Source LLC
Chambersburg PA
CBHW021528090426
42739CB00007B/831